STAR WARS

EPISODE II

TM

LUCAS
BOOKS

EBURY
PRESS

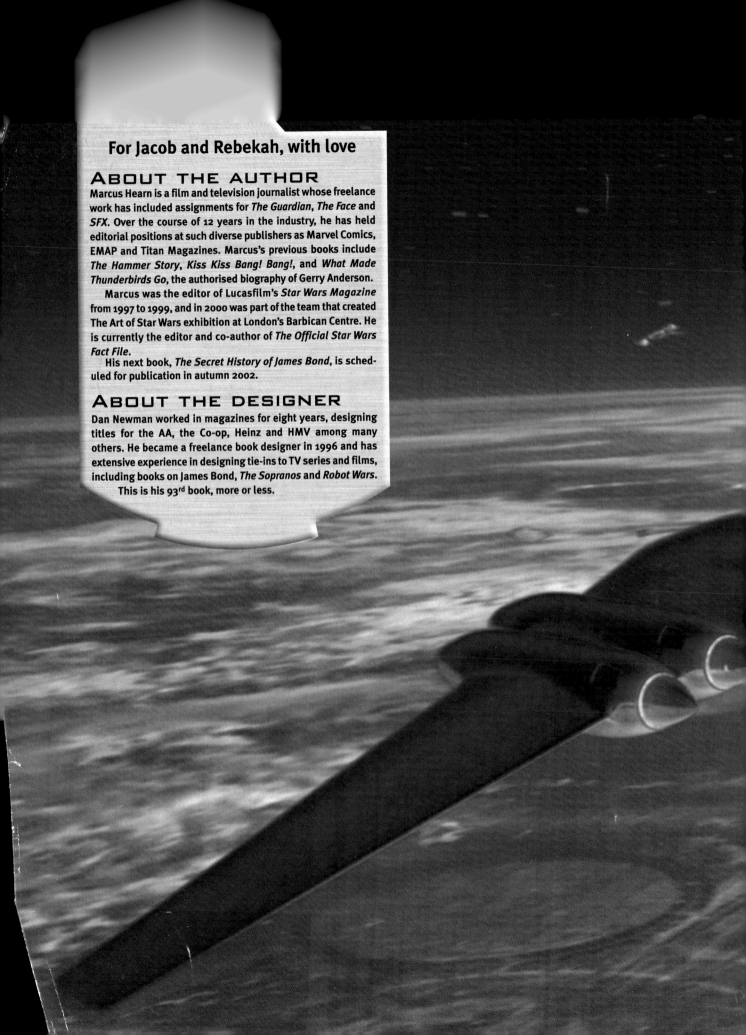

For Jacob and Rebekah, with love

ABOUT THE AUTHOR

Marcus Hearn is a film and television journalist whose freelance work has included assignments for *The Guardian*, *The Face* and *SFX*. Over the course of 12 years in the industry, he has held editorial positions at such diverse publishers as Marvel Comics, EMAP and Titan Magazines. Marcus's previous books include *The Hammer Story*, *Kiss Kiss Bang! Bang!*, and *What Made Thunderbirds Go*, the authorised biography of Gerry Anderson.

Marcus was the editor of Lucasfilm's *Star Wars Magazine* from 1997 to 1999, and in 2000 was part of the team that created The Art of Star Wars exhibition at London's Barbican Centre. He is currently the editor and co-author of *The Official Star Wars Fact File*.

His next book, *The Secret History of James Bond*, is scheduled for publication in autumn 2002.

ABOUT THE DESIGNER

Dan Newman worked in magazines for eight years, designing titles for the AA, the Co-op, Heinz and HMV among many others. He became a freelance book designer in 1996 and has extensive experience in designing tie-ins to TV series and films, including books on James Bond, *The Sopranos* and *Robot Wars*.

This is his 93rd book, more or less.

STAR WARS

EPISODE II

ATTACK OF THE CLONES
THE ILLUSTRATED COMPANION

Behind the Scenes and Inside the Story of Episode II

MARCUS HEARN

AT EBURY PRESS:
Editor: Marcus Hearn
Designer: Dan Newman/Perfect Bound

AT LUCASFILM:
Art Editor: Iain R. Morris
Editor: Jonathan W. Rinzler

The stills in this book were taken by Sue Adler, Albert Clarke, Keith Hamshere, John Jay, Paul Tiller, Lisa Tomasetti, Giles Westley, and George Whitear.

First published in Great Britain in 2002

1 3 5 7 9 10 8 6 4 2

Ebury Press
Random House
20 Vauxhall Bridge Road, London SW1V 2SA

The Random House Group Limited Reg. No. 954009

A CIP catalogue record for this book is available from the British Library.

www.starwars.com
www.randomhouse.co.uk

ISBN: 0 09 188478 0

Printed and bound in Germany by Mohn Media

Papers used by Ebury Press are natural, recyclable products made from wood grown in sustainable forests.

CONTENTS

A long time ago
in a galaxy far, fa

THE STORY SO FAR....

NINE-YEAR-OLD Anakin Skywalker is a slave on the planet Tatooine. Anakin possesses an unusual aptitude for engineering and lightning-fast reflexes, but it is not until he encounters a Jedi Master called Qui-Gon Jinn that Anakin discovers he is very special.

Qui-Gon arrives on Tatooine with his Padawan apprentice, Obi-Wan Kenobi, and their travelling companion Padmé Amidala – the Queen of Naboo incognito. Qui-Gon discovers that Anakin is unusually sensitive to the Force, the mysterious natural energy that binds the galaxy together. A Jedi's strength flows from the light side of the Force and is used to protect the weak and vulnerable. The dark side of the Force is embraced by those with evil and destructive ambitions.

Leaving his home-made droid, C-3PO, and his mother, Shmi, Anakin joins Qui-Gon, Obi-Wan and Padmé on a journey to the planet Coruscant, the home of the Jedi High Council and the Galactic Senate. Queen Amidala hopes that the Senate will help liberate her home planet, Naboo, which has been invaded by the armies of the greedy Trade Federation. Anakin grows fond of the 14-year-old Padmé, but events soon overtake them. On Coruscant, Jedi Masters Yoda and Mace Windu lead the High Council in rejecting Qui-Gon's application to train Anakin. 'He is too old,' concludes Mace Windu. 'There is already too much anger in him.'

Moreover, Padmé realises the Senate cannot help her, so she and her friends return to Naboo. Upon her arrival, she makes an alliance with the Gungans and launches a counter-attack on the Trade Federation. During the ensuing battle, Qui-Gon clashes with the sinister Darth Maul, who is a member of the Sith, an ancient cult that adheres to the dark side of the Force.

Even though the Naboo forces succeed in thwarting the Trade Federation's plans, Qui-Gon is killed by Maul, who in turn is cut down by a distraught Obi-Wan. On Coruscant, the Jedi Council is troubled by the re-emergence of the Sith, and suspect that Darth Maul was working alongside either a master or an apprentice.

The level of Jedi Knight is conferred upon Obi-Wan, who then carries out his master's dying wish by asking to take on Anakin as his Padawan learner. Master Yoda reluctantly gives his consent.

The Trade Federation and its odious Viceroy Nute Gunray leave Naboo, but the identity of the second mysterious Sith Lord remains a mystery.

Supreme Chancellor Palpatine, the newly elected head of the Galactic Senate, is aware that Anakin, who was instrumental in the victory, has great potential. 'We will watch your career with great interest,' he smiles, placing a guiding hand on the boy's shoulder....

away....

EPISODE II:
ATTACK OF THE CLONES

TEN YEARS after the Battle of Naboo, Padmé Amidala is now the Senator of Naboo. Supreme Chancellor Palpatine presides over an increasingly ineffectual Senate that is rife with corruption and troubled by a new threat: Thousands of star systems have pledged their support to a Separatist movement dedicated to establishing a new order. The Separatists are led by Count Dooku, a charismatic former Jedi who was once Qui-Gon Jinn's Master.

There is growing support for the establishment of a grand army to protect the Republic. The peace-loving Padmé is horrified by the idea, fearing that the creation of an army will lead directly to war with the Separatists.

Just after the Senator arrives on Coruscant to speak out against the formation of an army, Amidala's Royal Cruiser is destroyed by a saboteur's bomb. Chancellor Palpatine recommends that Obi-Wan Kenobi and Padawan Anakin Skywalker be assigned to protect Amidala from any further assassination attempts, and she reluctantly accepts the imposition of yet another bodyguard.

Seeing Padmé again after ten years has a profound effect on Anakin. The impudent trainee Jedi is overwhelmed by his feelings for her, and is angered when Obi-Wan reminds him to curtail his emotions. Jedi are forbidden to fall in love.

After another assassination attempt on Padmé, Yoda orders Obi-Wan to track down the culprit, and Anakin is given his first solo assignment: to protect Padmé and escort her to safety on Naboo. As the Padawan and his charge journey, Anakin is disturbed by a recurring nightmare that his mother is the victim of terrible suffering. The beauty and tranquility of Padmé's home planet offers a respite for the troubled young man, and Padmé soon warms to her companion.

Meanwhile, an assassin's saberdart leads Obi-Wan to Kamino, a planet renowned for its cloning technology. Obi-Wan discovers that a huge army of clones is being cultivated, supposedly at the behest of a member of the Jedi Council. The genetic model for the army is bounty hunter Jango Fett, who lives on the planet with his clone son, Boba.

When Obi-Wan meets Jango, the latter realises that the Jedi has tracked him from Coruscant to Kamino. Following a violent struggle with Obi-Wan, Jango and Boba flee Kamino in their spaceship, *Slave I*. Obi-Wan pursues them to the droid foundries on the planet Geonosis.

On Naboo, Anakin and Padmé fall in love – even though Padmé knows that such a relationship will make both their lives difficult. Anakin continues to be tormented by dreams of his mother, however, and feels compelled to return to Tatooine to seek her out. Padmé volunteers to accompany him.

Once on Tatooine, Anakin discovers that Shmi is no longer a slave, but is married to a moisture farmer who lives near Mos Eisley spaceport. When he and Padmé arrive at the farm, he finds out that his mother has been kidnapped by Tusken Raiders. Anakin borrows a swoop bike and resolves to find her. Padmé stays behind with her droid, R2-D2, and the droid Anakin had built as a young boy, C-3PO.

On Geonosis, it becomes clear that an alliance of powerful trade and guild clans are plotting a new order based on unlimited greed, which will be backed by a new army of Battle Droids. Obi-Wan discovers that they have a powerful ally in the shape of Jango Fett's paymaster – Count Dooku, the leader of the Separatists. Obi-Wan also finds out that the Trade Federation is behind the assassination attempts on Padmé.

Obi-Wan is captured by Dooku, who tells him that the Senate is gradually falling under the control of a powerful Sith Lord named Darth Sidious. Obi-Wan refuses to believe him.

Back on Tatooine, Anakin finds Shmi at a Tusken Raider camp moments before she dies of the wounds inflicted by her tormentors. Anakin gives in to his rage and ignites his lightsaber; he kills every Tusken man, woman, and child in revenge for the torture and death of his mother.

Anakin and Padmé, joined by R2-D2 and C-3PO, then head for Geonosis in an effort to rescue Obi-Wan. Anakin and Padmé are captured by winged Geonosians and soon join Obi-Wan in captivity. All three are condemned to public execution in a huge arena.

As Count Dooku and Nute Gunray gloat before their helpless prisoners, Supreme Chancellor Palpatine is given emergency powers and proceeds to sanction the use of the clone army to combat the Separatists' droid army. After a harrowing escape from beasts in the arena, Padmé, Anakin and Obi-Wan are about to meet their doom at the mechanical hands of droidekas, when Mace Windu and nearly two hundred Jedi suddenly arrive. A fierce combat between the Jedi and hundreds of Battle Droids ensues, yet the Jedi are overwhelmed by the sheer numbers of their opponents. Mace Windu kills Jango Fett, but Count Dooku orders the elimination of the surviving Jedi. The Jedi are saved only when the clone army comes to the rescue.

Dooku flees with Anakin and Obi-Wan in pursuit. In Dooku's hangar, the Count wounds both Jedi in a fierce duel. The diminutive Yoda arrives, however, and quickly overcomes Dooku, who takes flight in his Solar Sailer.

Anakin returns with Padmé to Naboo, where they are secretly married. Nevertheless, the Republic has taken a dark turn – the Clone Wars have begun.

And all the time, the sinister Darth Sidious skilfully manipulates events from the shadows.

Supreme Chancellor Palpatine tells Anakin, 'I see you becoming the greatest of all the Jedi.' But does Anakin posses the discipline to help save the Jedi Order?

The World of Episode II

Anakin Skywalker

His outstanding talent with a lightsaber and his unusual affinity with the Force are put to good use in the execution arena.

The Jedi Council is aware of Anakin's exceptional skills, and Mace Windu believes Anakin may fulfil the prophecy that says a being will one day bring balance to the Force. But Anakin still has a lot to learn....

THE SELFLESS nine-year-old who astonished the crowds at the Boonta Eve Classic Podrace has left Tatooine – and his mother – behind.

Anakin Skywalker is now 20 years old. Tatooine has become a distant memory for the restless young man and he dislikes being reminded of his boyhood nickname, 'Annie'.

Since the death of Qui-Gon Jinn, Anakin has come under the wing of father-figure Obi-Wan Kenobi. As Obi-Wan's Padawan, Anakin accompanies him on missions, learning and training to face the trials that will ultimately decide if he is worthy of becoming a Jedi Knight.

Anakin has retained his breathtaking abilities as a pilot – even if Obi-Wan considers him more than a little foolhardy when piloting an airspeeder through the crowded skies of Coruscant. Anakin has also become skilled with a lightsaber, although he often loses his weapon – for example, during a scuffle with bounty hunter Zam Wesell. Anakin built his first lightsaber at the age of 13, while in a trance, but Obi-Wan still has to remind his boisterous Padawan that it is his most valuable possession. It is one of many lessons the young apprentice has yet to learn.

Anakin's restless nature is beset by contradictions – he respects Obi-Wan but secretly resents the fact he has not been allowed to undertake the trials sooner. Anakin is also overwhelmed by the love he feels for Padmé, but frustrated first by shyness and later by his obligation to the Jedi Order.

Anakin also has difficulty appreciating Padmé's world of diplomacy and political negotiation. Moreover, he is plagued by nightmares about Shmi, the mother he left behind in slavery while he went to the Jedi Temple on Coruscant. Anakin yearns to be emotionally disciplined like a Jedi, but succumbs to rage when he discovers the terrible fate that has befallen his mother as a victim of Tusken Raiders.

Though Anakin falters, he remains full of good intentions. When Obi-Wan is taken prisoner on Geonosis, Anakin comes to his rescue.

BORN INTO SLAVERY

Anakin Skywalker had no father, but a devoted mother named Shmi who was a slave to the Toydarian spare parts dealer Watto. Jedi Master Qui-Gon Jinn won Anakin's freedom in a bargain he struck with Watto, but he could not secure the release of Shmi. Some years after Anakin left Tatooine with Qui-Gon, Watto sold Shmi to moisture farmer Cliegg Lars.

When Anakin returns to Tatooine, he finds Watto in rather reduced circumstances and asks him to help him locate his mother.

A DARK FUTURE

Anakin Skywalker's immediate destiny is unclear, but the distant future will see him undergo a terrible transformation. Anakin will forsake the Jedi, and pledge allegiance to their arch-enemies, the Sith. In the masked and cloaked guise of Darth Vader, Anakin is destined to become a ruthless Sith Lord who will brutally subjugate the galaxy for many years before finally being redeemed by his son – and one last desperate act.

'I will be
the most
powerful
Jedi ever!'

ANAKIN'S AIRSPEEDER

Airspeeders defy gravity with repulsorlift engines – relatively low-powered mechanisms that are built into numerous hovering vehicles and droids.

When Obi-Wan Kenobi is dragged off into the night sky clutching the fins of Zam Wesell's Assassin Droid, Anakin Skywalker sprints towards the nearby Senatorial parking zone and jumps into a bright yellow airspeeder. 'What took you so long?' asks Obi-Wan when Anakin rescues him. 'Oh, you know, Master,' jokes Anakin, 'I couldn't find a speeder I really liked – and then you know I had to get a really gonzo colour...'

When Obi-Wan joins Anakin in the passenger seat of the airborne hot-rod, he is grateful for the tractor units that keep him inside the vehicle during some of Anakin's more reckless manoeuvres.

IMPERIAL SPEEDERS

In the years following the Clone Wars, Imperial scout troopers will use specially adapted military speeder bikes for patrol and reconnaissance missions. Although not as fast as swoop bikes, vehicles such as the Aratech 74-Z are manoeuvrable enough to negotiate the dense Forest Moon of Endor.

OWEN'S SWOOP BIKE

Vaporators need to be set between 250 and 500 metres apart for optimum performance, and the more vaporators a moisture farm has the more credits it will earn. The devices need constant monitoring, as high technology of any kind is a potential target for Tusken Raiders, and condensed water is a highly prized commodity on Tatooine. Moisture farmers such as Owen Lars use swoop bikes – single-seat repulsorlift vehicles – to patrol the outer reaches of their land. At other times, the vehicles are used to haul water trailers or vermin traps.

Tatooine rarely gets the latest models because its position in the Outer Rim territories means it is too far away from the core planets' sales channels. Owen Lars' battered vehicle is around 40 years old, but would be regarded as relatively recent by his contemporaries. Despite its age and appearance, Owen prefers it to the other craft at his disposal because it is fuel-efficient and easy to repair using parts bought from the scavenging Jawas.

Although swoop bikes are notoriously difficult to manoeuvre, Anakin Skywalker has no hesitation in borrowing Owen's vehicle to use on his quest to find his abducted mother. Anakin was Tatooine's first human Podracing champion, and he has no problem handling a simple swoop bike.

In later years, landspeeders will also come into use on the Lars homestead. Luke Skywalker will use one such battered vehicle – which also operates on repulsorlift technology – to travel between his aunt and uncle's moisture farm and such destinations as Mos Eisley.

'I have more important things to do than fall in love.'

Padmé Amidala

PADMÉ NABERRIE served two four-year terms as elected Queen Amidala of Naboo, and proved so popular a ruler that her subjects reportedly wanted to amend the constitution so she could stay on.

Padmé could never have approved of such a measure – her belief in democracy is unshakeable and she is happy instead to serve as a Senator under her successor, Queen Jamillia.

Padmé's dedication to political life and her commitment to peaceful reform are at the heart of her opposition to the Military Creation Act. Padmé feels that the creation of an army – even if in response to the threat posed by Count Dooku's Separatists – will eventually lead to war.

Amidala is on her way to attend the Senate's vote on the Military Creation Act when an attempt is made on her life by a saboteur. Padmé's Royal Cruiser is destroyed and her devoted handmaiden, Cordé, is unwittingly killed as a decoy. The handmaiden apologises before dying in the arms of her distraught mistress.

Padmé's noble ideals and dedication to duty inspire similar loyalty from her family, who are proud of their daughter's selfless dedication but concerned that she has neglected her emotional well-being. Padmé's duties have indeed placed restrictions on her private life; her ambitions to have a family were put on hold when Queen Jamillia asked her to become a Senator.

Padmé's beliefs pose a threat to those who conspire against the Republic, and the resolution of the Battle of Naboo has left the bellicose Neimoidians with a score to settle against her. Even when Padmé's life is in danger, she objects to the Jedi bodyguards that Chancellor Palpatine imposes. She is feisty enough to stand up to Count Dooku's threats – both in the Galactic Senate and face-to-face – and is the first to escape the chains that bind her and her friends in the execution arena on Geonosis.

One of her bodyguards proves to be Anakin Skywalker, however.

The Young Queen

When Padmé was a child her history studies helped her realise that politicians could bring about change for the better.

She followed in her father's footsteps by working for the relief movement when she was very young. When she was 11, Padmé became an apprentice legislator, and then Princess of Theed, Naboo's capital city. By the time she was 14, she had been elected Queen of Naboo. The transformation from smiling schoolgirl to stern adolescent was complete.

As an adult, she has no regrets about devoting so much of her life to political service, though Padmé now feels she was too young for the responsibility of monarchy, and feels that the opportunity to have a family may be passing her by.

Padmé's mother, Jobal, and father, Ruwee, both feel that Padmé has dedicated enough of her life to politics and fear for her safety following the attempts on her life. Padmé also has an older sister, Sola, and two loveable nieces – Ryoo and Pooja.

The nine-year-old boy she first encountered on Tatooine is now a 20-year-old Padawan apprentice, and his intense feelings for his old friend prove to be the one thing Padmé is powerless to resist....

ROYAL STARSHIP

Queen Amidala's J-Type Royal Starship was better suited to diplomatic missions than the dangerous scenario of the Trade Federation's offensive against Naboo. The ship's shield generators were unable to repel a direct hit, which severely damaged the Nubian 327 engine. The Naboo Royal Cruiser's G-Type's engines have twice the thrust of its predecessor's, and more effective, all encompassing shields.

In the years following the Clone Wars, the Rebel Alliance will continue to use diplomacy as a means of resolving their differences with the Empire. Princess Leia Organa's consular ship is the Tantive IV, the blockade runner captured by Darth Vader en route to Tatooine.

NABOO ROYAL CRUISER

Although Padmé Amidala is no longer the Queen of Naboo, the G-type custom-built Royal Cruiser that carries her on diplomatic missions is every bit as impressive as the Royal Starship that took her into temporary exile ten years before.

The ship descends gracefully through the atmosphere of Coruscant and comes to rest near the Senate building, closely accompanied by three escorting N1 starfighters. Shortly after Padmé disembarks, a hidden bomb is detonated. The ensuing explosion destroys the ship and kills Padmé's decoy, Cordé.

NUBIAN YACHT

When Anakin and Padmé decide to go to Tatooine to find
Anakin's mother, they depart Naboo in a Nubian Yacht. Padmé
once again enjoys the privilege of travelling in a chromium-
plated starship. The yacht comes to rest in Mos Espa spaceport,
and is a distinguished addition to the less auspicious craft that
are also docked at Tatooine's notorious capital.

QUI-GON JINN

Qui-Gon Jinn was trained in the ways of the Force by eminent Jedi Master Dooku. Qui-Gon was a wise, noble Jedi in his own right when he encountered a remarkably Force-sensitive child called Anakin Skywalker on Tatooine. Qui-Gon Jinn freed Anakin from slavery with the aim of adopting him as his Padawan. Master Yoda had other ideas – the boy was too old and had the wrong temperament to be a Jedi. Qui-Gon was bitterly disappointed, and felt sure that under his tutelage the boy could follow in the footsteps of his current Padawan, Obi-Wan Kenobi.

Qui-Gon did not live long enough to see the future of the boy whose life he'd changed.

Obi-Wan Kenobi

OBI-WAN KENOBI was 25 standard years old when his master, Qui-Gon Jinn, was killed by a Sith assassin during the Battle of Naboo. It was Qui-Gon's dying wish that Obi-Wan should train Anakin Skywalker. Yoda had already argued that the nine-year-old was already too old to begin the training, but reluctantly gave his consent.

Ten years later, Obi-Wan is a fully fledged Jedi Knight, and the stresses of training the argumentative and reckless Anakin have made him wise and cynical beyond his years.

Obi-Wan and Anakin have recently returned from a border dispute on the planet Ansion when they are assigned to protect Senator Amidala. Obi-Wan clashes with his Padawan almost immediately – Anakin tells Padmé they will conduct an investigation into her recent assassination attempt, and Obi-Wan feels obliged to remind him that their orders simply specify that they are to protect the Senator.

When he is assigned to find those responsible for the attempts on Amidala's life, the cautious Obi-Wan employs a degree of lateral thinking alongside his Jedi skills. When the technological resources of the Jedi Archives Library fail him, Obi-Wan instead relies on his instincts and visits his old friend Dexter Jettster. This more traditional means of gaining information leads Obi-Wan to Kamino, and the discovery that the bounty hunter commissioned to kill Senator Amidala has been used as the genetic model for a huge clone army numbering well over a million troops.

Obi-Wan ingeniously conducts his investigation of the facilities on Kamino without arousing the suspicion of the cloners, but bounty hunter Jango Fett soon recognises him as a threat. Obi-Wan has to prove himself in close combat with Jango, and later as a pilot in a space confrontation between his starfighter and Jango's *Slave I*.

Unlike his Padawan, Obi-Wan never loses sight of his duties and obligations to the Jedi Order. His respect for Yoda, Mace Windu, and the other members of the Council is heartfelt.

It is in Mace Windu that Obi-Wan confides his fears about the headstrong Anakin. Kenobi understands that Anakin is confused and disturbed, and accepts that his Padawan may indeed have been too young to begin his training.

'You're going to be the death of me,' Obi-Wan tells Anakin. Neither can know that this light-hearted comment carries a tragic prescience....

OBI-WAN'S FUTURE

Despite Obi-Wan's best efforts to steer Anakin in the right direction, the boy is destined to turn to the dark side of the Force. The Jedi Order will all but collapse under the iron fist of Darth Vader, and Obi-Wan will spend much of his old age in retreat among the sand-dunes of Tatooine.

Obi-Wan emerges from his hermit-like existence only when he encounters Anakin's estranged son, Luke Skywalker, while the boy is out searching for R2-D2. Together they embark on a journey that leads Obi-Wan to his final confrontation with his former Padawan....

'You will learn
your place,
young one.'

STARFIGHTER

Obi-Wan Kenobi is given the crucial task of locating the bounty hunter responsible for the attempts on Senator Amidala's life. Obi-Wan's mission takes him to Kamino, and later to Geonosis. His transport to these destinations – and during a deep space duel on his way to the latter – is the wedge-shaped Delta-7 *Aethersprite* light interceptor.

The Delta-7 has a limited cargo capability, but Obi-Wan has some spare parts canisters on board when Jango Fett attempts to shoot him down on the approach to Geonosis. Obi-Wan ejects the canisters, and fools Jango into thinking he has destroyed the pursuing ship.

Obi-Wan relies on the navigational skills of Astromech Droid R4-P17, who is hard-wired into the port side of the ship. As well as assisting with navigation, R4 interfaces with the ship's computers to monitor and diagnose flight performance.

The Jedi starfighter might not be the fastest or most heavily armed ship in space, but it is elegant enough for a Jedi and small enough to hide on the dark side of an asteroid or beneath a rocky outcrop.

STAR DESTROYERS

The Delta-7 was developed by Kuat Systems Engineering, a subsidiary of Kuat Drive Yards. The Victory-class Star Destroyer, developed in the final years of the Old Republic, resembled a Delta-7 on a much larger scale. Kuat will remain in business following the demise of the Old Republic, and will go on to produce a number of other types of Star Destroyers, all of which retain the distinctive wedge-shaped design.

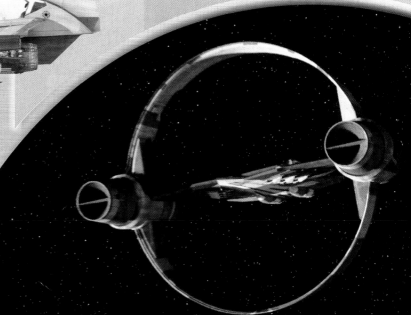

Unlike larger ships such as the *Millennium Falcon*, the Delta-7 is too small to be capable of lightspeed. When Obi-Wan makes his journey to Kamino, he uses the ship's hyperdrive booster ring, which affords the vessel's engine the performance of a class one hyperdrive. The Delta-7 disengages from the ring before it enters the planet's atmosphere.

THE SILVER-HAIRED and saturnine Count Dooku is a gentleman of the old school – but behind the courteous and well-mannered demeanour, he is engineering a conflict that will have terrible consequences for the galaxy.

Only 20 Jedi have ever renounced their Order. Of those 20, Dooku is the latest and the most powerful. Obi-Wan Kenobi learns much about Count Dooku from Jedi Archivist Jocasta Nu. She tells him that Count Dooku had much in common with the late Qui-Gon Jinn – he was an idealist and a very individual thinker who often found himself out of step with the Jedi Council. 'I think he left because he lost faith in the Republic,' says Jocasta. 'He believed that politics were corrupt, and he felt the Jedi betrayed themselves by serving the politicians.'

Dooku disappeared for nine or ten years, only to resurface as the charismatic leader of a Separatist movement that seeks to maximise the profits of its members by campaigning for lower taxes, reduced tariffs, and the eventual abolition of all trade barriers.

By the time Obi-Wan encounters Count Dooku on Geonosis, thousands of star systems have already rallied to his cause. Dooku is secretly joining forces with the Trade Federation, the Commerce Guild, and the InterGalactic Banking Clan in order to amass an army of Battle Droids so huge that the Republic will be overwhelmed.

Count Dooku's political abilities are impressive, but when Obi-Wan is forced to confront him he begins to understand why Jocasta Nu described Dooku's knowledge of the Force as 'unique'.

The Count asks both Obi-Wan and Padmé to join him in his revolution against the Republic. When they refuse, he

'It is time to start over.'

plans agonising and humiliating deaths for them both, and delights in their suffering before the jeering crowds in the execution arena on Geonosis.

Dooku is an expert old-style swordsman, and his ability with a lightsaber proves harrowing to Anakin and Obi-Wan, though not to the much wiser and more powerful Master Yoda.

Dooku escapes in his Solar Sailer. Yet even Dooku's evil ambitions and greedy new allies cannot compare to his shadowy master. Although Dooku skilfully brings the Republic to the brink of disaster, he is merely the instrument of a much greater evil....

NUTE GUNRAY

Count Dooku's most prominent ally is vile Neimoidian Nute Gunray, the Viceroy of the Trade Federation. Gunray is well known to Obi-Wan Kenobi as the prime mover behind the Trade Federation's audacious attempt to blockade and then invade Naboo.

Gunray still clings to power despite numerous hearings and four trials in which his corrupt dealings were exposed in the Supreme Court.

He is an enthusiastic supporter of Count Dooku, although for once he is not motivated purely by money. He knows that victory over the Republic will destroy everything Senator Amidala stands for, and he will not rest until he has the former Queen's head on his desk....

SOLAR SAILER

Sith Lord Count Dooku has renounced the Jedi, but is forced to confront some of its most proficient members during a gruelling lightsaber battle in his secret hangar on Geonosis.

Dooku proves more than a match for Obi-Wan and Anakin, but is beaten back by Yoda. He makes his escape from the planet aboard his Solar Sailer, a unique vehicle with a curious origin. A large sail unfurls from the bow of the ship as it leaves the atmosphere of Coruscant, and provides a mysterious source of energy for Dooku's journey. Before the ship reaches its destination, the sail withdraws into the body of the vessel. Like many of Dooku's possessions, the sail hearkens back to mysterious lore and lost technology.

DOOKU'S SPEEDER

Like Darth Maul, Count Dooku uses a compact repulsorlift vehicle as his personal transport. Both craft offer a useful combination of high speed and excellent visibility.

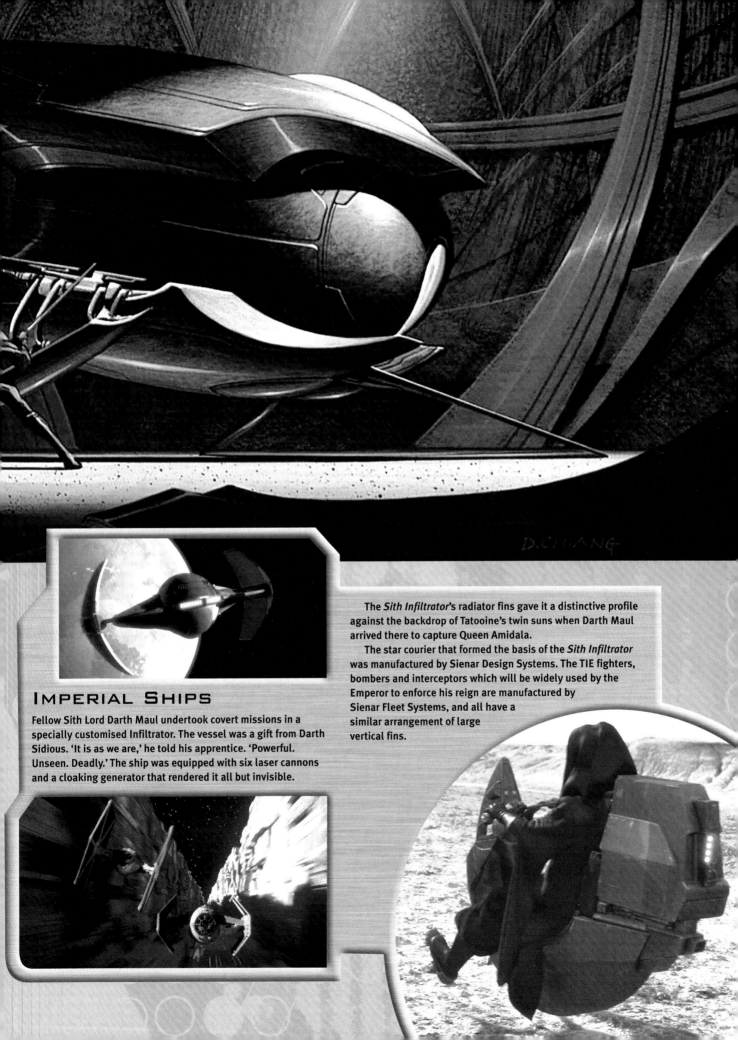

D. CHIANG

IMPERIAL SHIPS

Fellow Sith Lord Darth Maul undertook covert missions in a specially customised Infiltrator. The vessel was a gift from Darth Sidious. 'It is as we are,' he told his apprentice. 'Powerful. Unseen. Deadly.' The ship was equipped with six laser cannons and a cloaking generator that rendered it all but invisible.

The *Sith Infiltrator*'s radiator fins gave it a distinctive profile against the backdrop of Tatooine's twin suns when Darth Maul arrived there to capture Queen Amidala.

The star courier that formed the basis of the *Sith Infiltrator* was manufactured by Sienar Design Systems. The TIE fighters, bombers and interceptors which will be widely used by the Emperor to enforce his reign are manufactured by Sienar Fleet Systems, and all have a similar arrangement of large vertical fins.

SUPREME CHANCELLOR PALPATINE

The Supreme Chancellor is a man of peace caught in the heart of a unique conflict.

It is with great sadness that Palpatine informs the Galactic Senate that Senator Amidala has been assassinated. He is relieved to discover later that Padmé is in fact unharmed, although his concern for her safety leads him to suggest that Obi-Wan Kenobi should protect the Senator from any further attacks.

Such consideration is typical of this scholarly and very private politician. He seemed surprised when the blockade of Naboo thrust him into the political limelight. Since then, he has continued to campaign against corruption in the Senate, and has gained much support among his fellow legislators.

Palpatine is down to earth and modest; one of the few concessions to his position of authority are the audaciously clad red-robed guards who now accompany him.

While others lose faith in the Republic, Palpatine upholds his belief in the institution and reassures Mace Windu that the Republic will stand against the Separatists. He does, however, make a special point of enquiring exactly how many Jedi would be available for special duties should the conflict with the Separatists escalate into war.

Many claim the Senate is bogged down with bureaucracy and rife with corruption, but the events leading up to the Clone Wars show that Palpatine adheres to the approved procedures. When Palpatine is granted emergency powers to deal with the crisis on Geonosis, he is in no doubt about the correct course of action: He commissions a grand army of clone troopers to combat the swelling ranks of Battle Droids fighting for the Separatists.

After his victory on Geonosis, the Supreme Chancellor seems deep in sorrow as he watches tens of thousands of clone troopers board Republic assault ships, preparing to engage the Separatist forces throughout the galaxy in the ongoing Clone Wars.

'I love democracy... I love the Republic.'

SENATOR BAIL ORGANA

Senator Bail Organa is the head of the Royal Family of Alderaan and, like many people from his home planet, a committed pacifist.

An acknowledged cynic and realist, even Bail is fooled by the seemingly benevolent Supreme Chancellor Palpatine.

Bail's perception of his colleague and confidante Supreme Chancellor Palpatine may be reassessed during the Clone Wars. Bail is instrumental in rebuilding the battle-scarred Alderaan, and, according to some sources, deserves much of the credit for envisioning the Rebel Alliance.

When Anakin succumbs to the dark side, Obi-Wan Kenobi places Padmé Amidala in his care. Bail and his wife, Alderaan's Minister of Education, will later raise Leia, Anakin and Padmé's daughter, as if she was their own.

SENATOR PALPATINE

After many frustrating years in the political wilderness, Palpatine was elected to the Galactic Senate to represent his home planet, Naboo, and 35 other systems in the Outer Rim. Throughout decades of quiet perseverance, he gained the support of his fellow Senators, and even the Jedi Council came to regard him as a trusted and honourable politician. When Supreme Chancellor Valorum lost a vote of no-confidence during the crisis on Naboo, Senator Palpatine was perfectly placed for his next ascension to power. With the support of his friend and ally Queen Amidala, Palpatine was elected the new Supreme Chancellor. During the ensuing conflict between the Trade Federation and the peoples of Naboo, Palpatine proved that his mild exterior belied a steely resilience.

YODA

Well over 800 standard years old, Yoda is the most senior member of the Jedi High Council in every respect.

A wrinkled, green-skinned creature of unknown origin, Yoda presides over the 12-strong Jedi Council on Coruscant. The ultimate responsibility for the galaxy's thousands of Jedi resides with him, but he also finds time to take a personal interest in the training of Force-sensitive youngsters, and has personally supervised the apprenticeships of most young Padawans.

Yoda and his colleagues were alarmed when the appearance of assassin Darth Maul heralded the re-emergence of the Sith. The Sith are a diabolical cult that embraces the dark side of the Force, and were founded over five millennia ago. They were thought extinct until Darth Maul attacked Qui-Gon Jinn on Tatooine.

Yoda was wise enough to know that Maul must have been working with a partner – either a master or an apprentice – and that his death did not mark the end of the Sith threat. Since the appearance of Darth Maul, Yoda has been wondering when the Sith would re-emerge; as the Republic is once more threatened, he is beset with a growing feeling of unease.

Unfortunately, a disturbance in the Force masks Yoda's ability to see into the future, and, as the chaos created by the Separatists spreads, he is forced to act without his usual powers of foresight.

Yoda's allies include his right hand man, Master Mace Windu, and Supreme Chancellor Palpatine, to whom he reveals how thinly stretched the Jedi are.

Yoda also has the utmost respect for Obi-Wan Kenobi, and therefore assigns him the important task of tracking down the armoured assassin behind the attempts on the life of Senator Amidala. Yoda may be less wise to place his trust in Obi-Wan's Padawan, Anakin Skywalker, whom he orders to protect Padmé Amidala.

When Obi-Wan's investigations point to an elusive planet called Kamino, Yoda enlists the help of some of his youngest Padawans and asks them why the planet doesn't appear on the star-map hologram.

'The shroud of the dark side has fallen.'

Unlike Jedi Archives custodian Jocasta Nu, Yoda is open-minded enough to accept one child's opinion that the records could have been altered. Yoda expresses grave concern over the situation – only a Jedi could have tampered with the Archives in such a way.

After Obi-Wan's investigation leads to Geonosis and the discovery of a massive droid army, Yoda goes to Kamino and commandeers the clone army. During the resultant horrific battle on the red planet, Yoda confronts renegade Jedi Count Dooku, the leader of the Separatists and the droid army. The two begin by powerfully manipulating the Force and then duelling with lightsabers – but the Count is no match for Yoda, and flees in his Solar Sailer.

'A Jedi uses the Force for knowledge,' Yoda often tells his Padawans, 'never for attack.' But a war that threatens the Republic and its Jedi protectors is looming, and Yoda knows that conflict is now inevitable.

JEDI TRAINING

When Obi-Wan Kenobi visits Master Yoda on the training veranda at the Jedi Temple, he is supervising a group of children aged between four and eight. Yoda refers to the children as 'the mighty Bear Clan', and he watches over them as they attempt to strike Training Droids with their miniature lightsabers. Yoda guides the children in the ways of the Force, but also recognises that their unfettered young minds may solve the mystery of the 'missing' planet Kamino.

Following the dissolution of the Jedi, Yoda will retreat to the Dagobah system and eke out a solitary existence in a mud hut. In the last few years of his life he will take on one final apprentice – Anakin's son, Luke Skywalker.

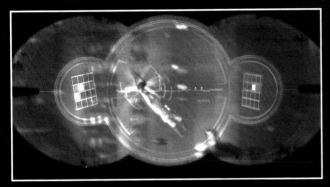

A HUNDRED STORIES above the streets of Coruscant, Obi-Wan hangs on to the Assassin Droid that has attempted to eliminate Senator Amidala. The droid carries Obi-Wan on a precarious high-speed journey towards bounty hunter Zam Wesell.

Zam reaches for a long rifle and takes aim as the droid approaches. One shot later, the droid takes a direct hit. It explodes, and Obi-Wan drops like a stone. He tumbles out of the sky – and lands in the cockpit of an airspeeder piloted by Anakin Skywalker.

Zam leaps into her own airspeeder, then flies into a tunnel, weaving in and out of oncoming traffic, and through a power refinery.

Just when Obi-Wan and Anakin think their quarry has evaded them, Anakin suddenly jumps out of their speeder, plunging hundreds of metres before landing on Zam's airspeeder.

'I hate it when he does that,' says his exasperated Master.

'I have a
bad feeling
about this.'

'This party's over.'

Mace Windu

ALTHOUGH HE IS a senior member of the Jedi Council, little in Mace Windu's experience has prepared him for the looming threats of the dark side of the Force and Count Dooku's Separatists.

Mace Windu's faith in the Jedi to protect the Republic is admirable, but it also blinds him to the true scale of the growing menace. He is aware that the dark side is growing, but still allows himself to be too easily reassured about the Separatists' ambitions. He over-estimates Anakin Skywalker, paying little credence to Obi-Wan's protestations that the boy is too confused and disturbed to be dispatched on a solo mission. And Mace fatally misjudges Count Dooku, refusing to believe he could be behind any attempt on Senator Amidala's life. 'Dooku was once a Jedi,' he tells Padmé. 'He couldn't assassinate anyone. It's not in his character.'

Mace Windu believes in the Jedi as keepers of the peace – not as soldiers – but there comes a point when he reluctantly realises that it is time to take affairs out of the realm of diplomacy. He takes all the Jedi he can muster to Geonosis, where he engages the sinister Count Dooku and bounty hunter Jango Fett.

Mace Windu's strengths are, in many ways, qualities shared by the Jedi Order as a whole – he is an accomplished diplomat and a fine swordsman. Such skills have served the Jedi well in their role as the galaxy's peacekeepers for a thousand generations. But such skills are not enough to save the Jedi from their own complacency, and the tumultuous changes that threaten to wipe them out forever.

SHMI SKYWALKER

Anakin has had no contact with his mother since his wrenching departure from Tatooine ten years ago. Plagued by nightmares in which Shmi is enduring terrible suffering, Anakin feels compelled to return to his home planet and seek her out.

Anakin has no father, and the unusually high concentration of midi-chlorians in his bloodstream point to the possibility that he was conceived by the will of the Force itself.

Shmi was a slave, and struggled to bring up her son in the face of extreme poverty. Qui-Gon Jinn won Anakin's freedom, but Shmi remained the property of a greedy Toydarian scrap dealer named Watto. Five years before Anakin's return to Tatooine, Watto sold Shmi to a moisture farmer called Cliegg Lars. Cliegg had fallen in love with Shmi and purchased her in order to free and then marry her.

A month before Anakin's arrival at the Lars' homestead, however, Shmi went to collect the mushrooms that grew on the vaporators, the devices that condense water vapour from the arid planet's air. She never came back.

Shmi was snatched by a hunting party of Tusken Raiders, savage creatures who make their home in the harsh desert environment of Tatooine's Jundland Wastes. Cliegg joined a search party numbering 30 people, but the Tusken Raiders were waiting and only four returned. The seriously injured Cliegg now believes that Shmi is lost forever, but Anakin is determined to find her.

Nothing can prepare Anakin for the shock of his reunion with his mother, and nothing can prepare the Tusken Raiders for Anakin's vengeful retribution....

'I missed you so much...'

'This isn't the way I wanted to meet you, son.'

THE LARS FAMILY

Rural moisture farming in the remote flatland regions of Tatooine is an isolated and often dangerous career. Moisture farmers use devices called vaporators – totem-like structures comprising rods and refrigerated cylinders – to draw moisture from Tatooine's atmosphere. Vaporators condense the surrounding air and store the water in collection chambers. The water is then filtered and pumped into underground tanks for consumption, irrigation, or sale.

Cliegg Lars owns a moisture farm relatively near Mos Eisley spaceport. Under the punishing glare of Tatooine's two suns, Cliegg and his son Owen toil to earn a modest living. After Anakin left Tatooine, Cliegg met and married Shmi Skywalker. Shmi has come to regard Owen as her own son, and has grown similarly fond of Owen's girlfriend, Beru Whitesun.

Moisture farmers live under the constant threat of violence from marauding Tusken Raiders. When Shmi is kidnapped by a party of Raiders, Cliegg attempts to rescue her and loses a leg in the ensuing struggle. When Anakin arrives at the Lars homestead in search of his mother, Cliegg is recovering from his injuries. He refuses to wear a mechanical replacement leg and instead gets around on a hovering power chair constructed by Owen.

Cliegg and Shmi had both looked forward to the day when Anakin returned to Tatooine, but Cliegg is sad to report that he doesn't think Shmi could have survived a month in the captivity of such barbaric creatures.

'I feel her pain,' insists Anakin, 'and I will find her.' Owen offers Anakin the use of his swoop bike, and an anxious Padmé stays with the Lars family while Anakin rides off into the inhospitable landscape of Tatooine.

When he returns, he brings Shmi's lifeless body with him. Cliegg conducts his wife's funeral with dignity, but neither he nor his newfound stepson will ever be the same again.

C-3PO AND R2-D2

'Oh, my circuits!' exclaims Protocol Droid C-3PO on seeing Anakin and Padmé, 'I'm so pleased to see you both!'

Anakin began constructing C-3PO when he was just nine years old. He hoped the droid would be able to assist his mother around the home, but C-3PO proved just as helpful when Shmi became the wife of a moisture farmer. Protocol Droids are especially useful on moisture farms as they can translate the programming languages employed by vaporators – in particular the binary language Bocce.

Anakin left Tatooine before he got the opportunity to put the finishing touches to C-3PO. Two years after Anakin left, Shmi fitted the embarrassed droid's exposed circuitry and mechanisms with a haphazard set of coverings.

When Anakin and Padmé unexpectedly find C-3PO on Tatooine, they take him with them on their way to Geonosis. The droid soon rekindles an unlikely companionship with Padmé's Astromech Droid, R2-D2.

Despite their bickering, the two are destined to become friends and companions over the coming years.

OWEN AND BERU

Owen Lars and Beru Whitesun will marry and make Cliegg's moisture farm their home until the ends of their lives. When Anakin succumbs to the dark side, his twin children – Leia and Luke – are separated and hidden for their safety. Leia will be adopted by Senator Bail Organa of Alderaan, and Luke will go to live with his Uncle Owen and Aunt Beru on the same moisture farm his father had visited years before when searching for his mother.

ZAM WESELL

BOUNTY HUNTERS

The appellation 'bounty hunter' carries a mystique that many fail to live up to. Many bounty hunters struggle to earn a living. The very best are smart enough to have their dirty work done by less experienced killers who are prepared to take risks to earn a reputation for themselves.

Bounty hunters thrive where law enforcement is inadequate, and as the Republic reels from growing corruption, many such mercenaries literally make a killing. Later, Imperial leaders and crime lords will encourage such notorious characters as Greedo, Bossk, Dengar, IG-88, and, of course, Boba Fett – the son of Jango.

ON A SKYSCRAPER ledge high above the bustling streets of Coruscant, a sinister rendezvous takes place. Bounty hunter Jango Fett, his features obscured by distinctive helmet and armour, meets his ruthless hired hand – fellow bounty hunter Zam Wesell.

Jango and Zam have collaborated before, most notably when they delivered an idol into the hands of an Annoo-Dat terrorist. The idol turned out to be a deadly weapon and the two joined forces to prevent a cataclysm on Coruscant. Zam has also been a friend to Jango's clone son, Boba Fett.

There is no room for conscience or moral responsibility during their latest assignment – Jango tells Zam his client is getting impatient, and Zam is prepared to dedicate her unerring skill to the job in hand in return for an appropriate fee.

Zam Wesell is a Clawdite – a changeling with the ability to alter her appearance at will. She is sub-contracted by Jango Fett to undertake the attempts on Padmé Amidala's life. It is Zam's ASN-121 Assassin

Droid that cuts open the window of Padmé's apartment, then releasing lethal kouhuns that make for the Senator while she sleeps.

Alerted to Padmé's danger, Obi-Wan grabs hold of the droid and clings to its dorsal fins during a hair-raising flight through Coruscant. Zam is determined not to be caught, and flees both Anakin and Obi-Wan in her airspeeder, despite some impressive and highly dangerous flying by the younger Jedi.

Zam's speeder grinds to a halt in a shower of sparks on the pavements of Coruscant, and she disappears into the teeming crowd of alien low-lifes, panhandling droids, and upper-class slummers.

Zam has the experience and physio-logical talents to blend in perfectly with a crowd, so she ducks into the Outlander gambling club. She quietly observes Obi-Wan as he orders a drink at the bar, and silently draws her blaster from her holster. But her skills as a hired killer are no match for the sixth sense possessed by a Jedi Knight. Obi-Wan detects her presence behind him and slices off her blaster arm with his lightsaber.

As life fades from Zam outside the club, Obi-Wan and Anakin question her. She admits that the target of her assassination attempt was Senator Amidala, but before she can reveal who paid her, a toxic saberdart from an armoured assailant ends her life.

'It was just a job.'

'We'll just
have to
finish him.'

JANGO FETT

JANGO FETT was orphaned at an early age and taken in by Jaster Mereel and the Mandalorians. Jango trained with their nomadic army, and after they were wiped out by the Jedi, Jango fought on alone – working for the highest bidder and still wearing the armour distinctive to his adopted homeland.

Jango is a frightening spectacle, in or out of his Mandalorian armour. His face is pitted with the scars of old wounds, and his muscular forearms bear a number of strange tattoos.

Jango was already renowned as the finest bounty hunter in the galaxy when he was approached by the mysterious Lord Tyranus on one of the moons of Bogden. Tyranus made Fett an offer he couldn't refuse, and, before long, the bounty hunter had agreed to relocate to Tipoca City on Kamino.

Jango allowed himself to be cloned by the Kaminoans, who used his genetic model to create an army of genetically modified troopers apparently commissioned by Jedi Master Sifo-Dyas on behalf of the Republic.

Jango was handsomely paid, and lives in comfort on Tipoca, free to come and go as he pleases on the condition he helps train the clone army. In addition, Jango made one further demand of the Kaminoans – an unaltered clone of himself whom he named Boba.

Jango emerges from Kamino only when the price is right, occasionally collaborating with Zam Wesell on especially demanding missions. Boba had given Jango a good reason to stay alive, and he was now content for Zam to risk her neck on his behalf.

Obi-Wan Kenobi first encounters Jango Fett when the rocket man swoops into the smog-filled sky of Coruscant after killing Zam Wesell with a toxic saberdart. Jango has a reputation for ruthlessness towards victims that extends to expendable colleagues such as Zam.

He subsequently proves himself powerful in close combat with Obi-Wan, who struggles to overcome the well-equipped warrior after tracing him back to Kamino. Jango's armour bristles with weaponry and gadgets, including retractable wrist-blades, a snare, and a rocket-firing jetpack. Luckily, Obi-Wan has a few gadgets of his own, and the tracking device he attaches to the hull of Fett's ship enables him to follow the bounty hunter.

On Geonosis, Obi-Wan discovers the bounty hunter's true master: former Jedi Master, Count Dooku. Eventually, Jango Fett pays the price for his chosen profession.

BOBA FETT

Jango's clone son flees Kamino with his father when Obi-Wan's investigations come close to revealing the truth. Although only ten years old, Boba is capable of operating *Slave I*'s on-board weapons in an effort to defend his father from Obi-Wan, and is an able co-pilot on the way to Geonosis. Boba's recognition of the Jedi starfighter's silhouette tells his father that they are being tracked by Obi-Wan.

After Jango's death at the hands of Mace Windu, Boba inherits more than just his father's battle-scarred helmet and armour – in the years following the Clone Wars, he will become in turn one of the most notorious and highly paid mercenaries in the galaxy.

SLAVE I

Obi-Wan Kenobi first sees Jango Fett's spaceship, *Slave I*, when Jango's son prepares it for lift-off from the landing platform at Tipoca City. Following a duel with Jango, Obi-Wan attaches a tracking device to the hull of *Slave I* before it leaves Kamino's stormy atmosphere. Obi-Wan follows the ship into deep space and into the perilous asteroid belts encircling Geonosis.

Slave I may appear unique because of its distinctive shape, but it started life as a Kuat Systems Engineering *Firespray*-class police vessel. The advanced technology on board is not restricted to the weaponry. Boba detects that Obi-Wan is following *Slave I* through space when he spots a cloaking silhouette on the flight deck's surveillance equipment. Jango pilots his ship into the asteroid field surrounding Geonosis, deftly flying the agile craft through a narrow tunnel in one of the larger rocks.

BOBA'S SLAVE I

Following the death of Jango Fett, Boba will become the sole pilot of *Slave I* and give the ship a distinctive new livery. The unmistakable *Slave I* becomes almost as notorious as its ruthless bounty-hunting owner, and is the means by which Boba transports the captured Han Solo from Bespin to Tatooine.

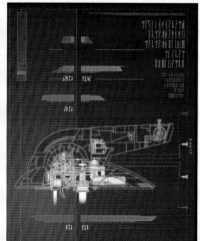

JOCASTA NU

Obi-Wan's friend Dexter Jettster explains that the toxic saberdart that killed Zam Wesell originated on Kamino, a planet of reclusive cloners located beyond the Outer Rim.

Obi-Wan has never heard of Kamino, so he decides to research the planet further in the Archives Library at the Jedi Temple. Madame Jocasta Nu, the Jedi Archivist, is elderly and frail-looking, but retains a sprightly demeanour and a caustic temperament. She cares for the Holocrons, repositories of Jedi instruction and teaching stretching back to the inception of the Order. Jocasta also presides over the library's more accessible holobooks, which also contain a wealth of information on Jedi history and culture.

Jocasta Nu readily shares her knowledge of former Jedi Count Dooku with Obi-Wan, but is mystified when he asks her about Kamino. She initiates a star-map hologram on a

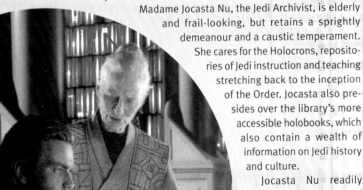

A SITH HOLOCRON

A few standard years before the Trade Federation's invasion of Naboo, Qui-Gon Jinn and a young Obi-Wan Kenobi followed the dangerous Sith expert, Dr Lundi, to the planet Kodai where lay – under tons of ocean water – a fabled Sith Holocron. Lundi hoped to acquire the artifact during the planet's low tide, which occurs only once every ten years. His plans were foiled by rivals, however, and the Holocron remained hidden.

Ten years later, Obi-Wan and his own Padawan, Anakin Skywalker, took up the chase with a now insane Dr Lundi as their guide. Obi-Wan and Anakin recovered the Sith Holocron, which is now stored in the care of Jocasta Nu in the Jedi Archives.

view screen, but the planet does not appear. She is unimpressed by the vague location offered by Dexter Jettster. 'It sounds like the sort of directions you'd get from a street tout,' she sniffs, 'some old miner or Furbog trader.' She concludes by telling Obi-Wan that Kamino does not actually exist.

Although well-meaning, Jocasta would be wise to be less reliant on technology as the sole source of her information. Her attitude says much about the stagnation that makes the Jedi so vulnerable in these uncertain times.

DARTH SIDIOUS

His features all but obscured beneath a black hood, Darth Sidious maintained a shadowy presence during the blockade of Naboo, pulling the strings of the weak-minded Trade Federation members and slowly but inexorably edging the galaxy toward war.

Sidious is a Dark Lord of the Sith, a practitioner of an evil cult that embraces the dark side of the Force. On several occasions in ancient galactic history, the Sith came close to eradicating the Jedi, but eventually they went into forced hiding and, to ensure their survival, they decided to keep their numbers down to only two. The Jedi Council were thus surprised by the appearance of Darth Maul, and his death was believed to have left just one other Sith – either Maul's master or apprentice.

Sidious retreated back into the shadows after the death of Maul, and patiently plotted his next move. Much later, on Geonosis, Count Dooku tells a disbelieving Obi-Wan Kenobi that hundreds of Senators have already fallen under the influence of Darth Sidious. 'You must join me,' he urges Obi-Wan, 'and together we will destroy the Sith.'

Dooku's motives are far from pure, and Obi-Wan is correct in assuming that Dooku's allegiance no longer lies with the High Council.

A disturbance in the Force hints of the presence of Darth Sidious, who watches and waits as the fabric of the galaxy is torn apart by his evil machinations.

'Everything is going as planned.'

DARTH MAUL

Just as Qui-Gon nurtured his Padawan Obi-Wan, Darth Sidious had an apprentice of his own. Darth Maul struck fear into his enemies, and his dexterity with a double-bladed lightsaber made him a formidable opponent.

Maul first attacked on Tatooine, then later killed Qui-Gon Jinn during the Battle of Naboo. A distraught Obi-Wan launched a ferocious counter-attack minutes later, using his dying Master's lightsaber to slice Maul in two.

Kenobi's surprise attack left a look of shock on Maul's face – apparent even as the villain plunged to the bottom of a cavernous pit.

PLANETS

TATOOINE

Tatooine's strategic location at the nexus of several hyperspace trade routes makes it a popular stop-off for merchants and smugglers, but virtually nobody else. There is little to attract visitors to this sparsely populated planet, where the midday temperature can exceed 65.5 °C and slavery is legal. One of the more legitimate pursuits on Tatooine is moisture farming, but those prepared to brave the inhospitable climate also face the threat of Tusken Raiders, nomadic savages that roam the dune seas. Tatooine is the adopted home of Shmi Skywalker and her remarkable son Anakin, who first lived there in slavery.

CORUSCANT

This densely populated planet lies at galactic co-ordinates zero-zero-zero on standard navigation charts. Tens of thousands of years of industrial and cultural growth have taken their toll on Coruscant, and there are hardly any areas of land that have not been developed – and over-developed. Coruscant is home to the Jedi Council and the Galactic Senate, but these centres for peaceful debate stand in stark contrast to the bustling skylanes clogged with speeding air traffic. The dark streets below the towering buildings are similarly packed with low-life and thrill seekers.

NABOO

A lush world of breathtaking natural beauty that lies within the Mid Rim, this geologically unique planet is inhabited by the Naboo on the surface, and the amphibious Gungans below swamp level. There are huge contrasts between the architecture of the two species: the Naboo govern from majestic splendour in the capital, Theed, while the Gungan seat of power is Otoh Gunga, an organic underwater city housed within huge hydrostatic bubbles. Famous Naboo residents include Padmé Amidala, once an elected Queen now a Senator, and Supreme Chancellor Palpatine, who spends much of his time on Coruscant.

GEONOSIS

A craggy, desolate planet that has been ravaged by cosmic ray storms. The inhabitants of this Outer Rim world have created awesome cathedral-like caverns to house their droid foundries. Geonosis's chief export is the Battle Droid which, in all its various models and specifications, is the chief foot soldier and cannon fodder for the Trade Federation and other guilds. Although governed by a strict work ethic, Geonosians emerge from their hives to enjoy the planet's most popular entertainment: open-air gladiatorial combat in the vast public arena.

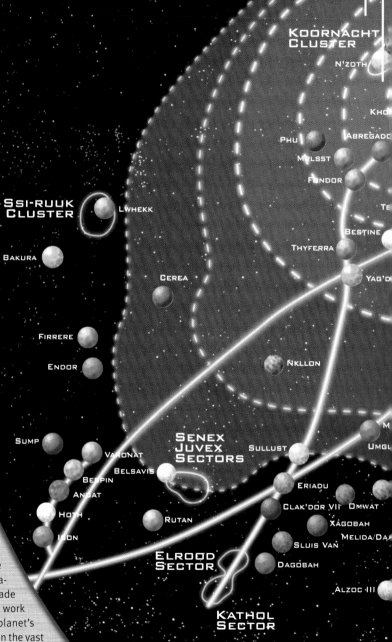

DEEP CORE
CORE WORLDS
COLONIES
INNER RIM
EXPANSION REGION
OUTER RIM

UNKNOWN REGIONS

KOORNACHT CLUSTER

N'ZOTH

KHO

PHU   ABREGADO

MRLSST

FONDOR

SSI-RUUK CLUSTER   LWHEKK

TE

BAKURA   BESTINE

CEREA   THYFERRA

YAG'D

FIRRERE

ENDOR   NKLLON

SUMP   SENEX   SULLUST   M
             JUVEX
VARONAT   SECTORS   UMGU
BELSAVIS
BESPIN   ERIADU
ANDAT
HOTH   RUTAN   CLAK'DOR VII OMWAT
ISON   XAGOBAH
                              MELIDA/DA
ELROOD   SLUIS VAN
SECTOR   DAGOBAH

                              ALZOC III
KATHOL
SECTOR

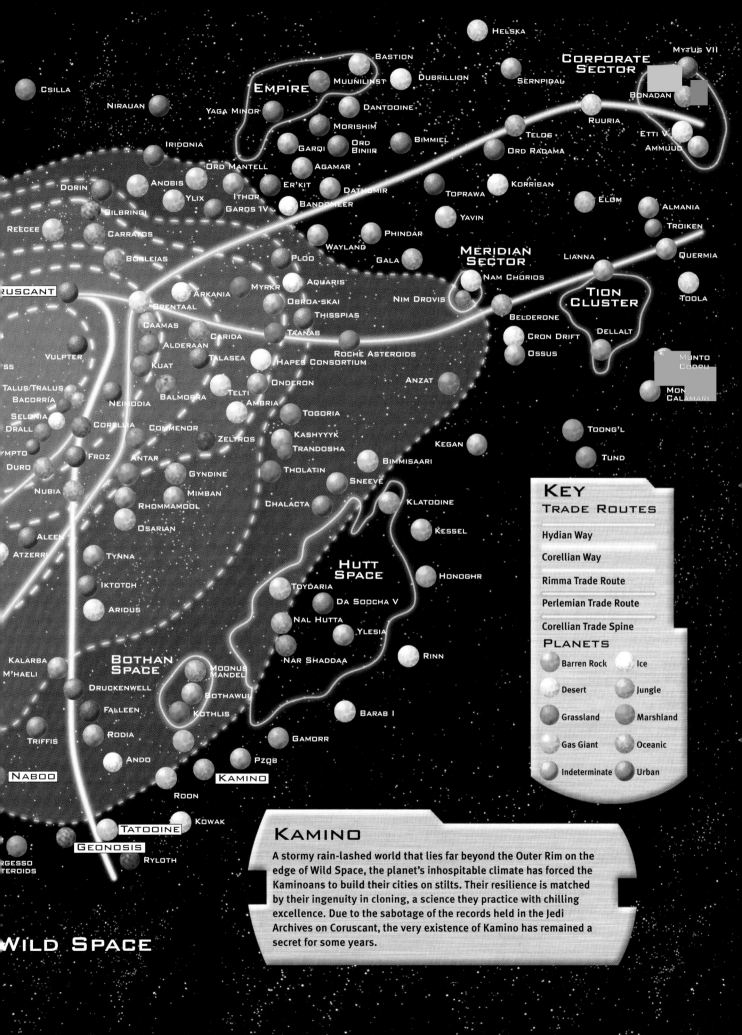

CSILLA

NIRAUAN

HELSKA

BASTION

MUUNILINST

DUBRILLION

EMPIRE

SERNPIDAL

CORPORATE
SECTOR

MYTUS VII

BONADAN

YAGA MINOR

DANTOOINE

RUURIA

ETTI V

IRIDONIA

MORISHIM

AMMUUD

DORIN

GARQI

ORD
BINIIR

BIMMIEL

TELOS

ORD RADAMA

ANOBIS

ORD MANTELL

AGAMAR

ELOM

ALMANIA

BILBRINGI

YLIX

ITHOR

ER'KIT

DATHOMIR

TOPRAWA

KORRIBAN

TROIKEN

RE'ECEE

CARRATOS

GAROS IV

BANDOMEER

YAVIN

CARRATOS

PHINDAR

QUERMIA

RUSCANT

BORLEIAS

ARKANIA

PLOO

WAYLAND

GALA

MERIDIAN
SECTOR

LIANNA

TOOLA

SPRENTAAL

MYRKR

AQUARIS

NAM CHORIOS

TION
CLUSTER

CAAMAS

OBROA-SKAI

NIM DROVIS

BELDERONE

DELLALT

VULPTER

ALDERAAN

CARIDA

THISSPIAS

CRON DRIFT

MUNTO
CODRU

SS

KUAT

TAANAB

OSSUS

TALUS/TRALUS

TALASEA

ROCHE ASTEROIDS

MON
CALAMARI

BACORRIA

BALMORRA

HAPES CONSORTIUM

SELONIA

NEIMODIA

TELTI

ONDERON

ANZAT

DRALL

AMBRIA

TOONG'L

CORELLIA

COMMENOR

TOGORIA

YMPTO

FROZ

ZELTROS

KASHYYYK

TUND

DURO

ANTAR

TRANDOSHA

KEGAN

NUBIA

GYNDINE

THOLATIN

BIMMISAARI

MIMBAN

SNEEVE

ALEEN

RHOMMAMOOL

CHALACTA

KLATOOINE

ATZERRI

OSARIAN

KESSEL

TYNNA

HONOGHR

IKTOTCH

HUTT
SPACE

ARIDUS

TOYDARIA

DA SOOCHA V

NAL HUTTA

YLESIA

RINN

KALARBA

NAR SHADDAA

M'HAELI

BOTHAN
SPACE

MOONUS
MANDEL

DRUCKENWELL

BOTHAWUI

FALLEEN

KOTHLIS

BARAB I

RODIA

GAMORR

TRIFFIS

ANDO

PZOB

NABOO

KAMINO

ROON

KOWAK

TATOOINE

GEONOSIS

RGESSO
TEROIDS

RYLOTH

WILD SPACE

KEY
TRADE ROUTES

Hydian Way

Corellian Way

Rimma Trade Route

Perlemian Trade Route

Corellian Trade Spine

PLANETS

Barren Rock   Ice

Desert   Jungle

Grassland   Marshland

Gas Giant   Oceanic

Indeterminate   Urban

KAMINO

A stormy rain-lashed world that lies far beyond the Outer Rim on the edge of Wild Space, the planet's inhospitable climate has forced the Kaminoans to build their cities on stilts. Their resilience is matched by their ingenuity in cloning, a science they practice with chilling excellence. Due to the sabotage of the records held in the Jedi Archives on Coruscant, the very existence of Kamino has remained a secret for some years.

TATOOINE

The Tatoo System lies in the Arkanis Sector of the Outer Rim. Tatooine bakes under the scorching glare of twin suns, and is justifiably condemned as an inhospitable and lawless dustbowl.

Tatooine is largely beyond the reach of the Republic, and is ruled by gangsters such as Jabba Desilijic Tiure – better known as Jabba the Hutt. Although slavery is illegal in Republic territories, it is permissible in Hutt Space; and the Hutts rule Tatooine.

The frequent sandstorms often erase natural features, making it difficult to compile reliable maps, but Tatooine's most notable landmarks are its spaceports. One of the best known is Mos Eisley in the Great Mesra Plateau. Once described by Obi-Wan Kenobi as 'a wretched hive of scum and villainy' the city of Mos Eisley has so many docking bays that it is considered a spaceport in its entirety. The oldest part of

the city is laid out in a central wheel shape, with newer buildings arranged in straight blocks. In common with much of the crude architecture on Tatooine, the buildings in Mos Eisley are rough adobe structures, half-buried in the ground to protect their occupants from the searing heat and frequent sandstorms.

Tatooine's largest city and default capital is the spaceport Mos Espa, on the lip of the Dune Sea. Mos Espa was home to slaves Anakin and Shmi Skywalker when they were owned by spare parts dealer Watto. Anakin worked in Watto's workshop and Shmi worked in his home. Both eked out a frugal existence in their tiny hovel in Mos Espa's densely populated slave quarter.

The marketplace at Mos Espa is a busy street where Shmi bought such local produce as Haroun bread, Tezirett seeds and Driss pods. Droid mechanics and other engineers keep cooling units near their wares, and street cafés offer refreshments to travellers.

Mos Espa is perhaps best known for its arena, which holds more than 100,000 spectators and is situated between the Northern Dune Sea and the Xelric Draw. The venue hosts such thrilling events as the Boonta Eve Classic Podrace, in which Anakin Skywalker won the historic victory that earned him his freedom.

For those who choose to earn a more legitimate living than the Hutts or the Podracing gamblers, there is the arduous career of

moisture farming. Tatooine has little rain and no running water; the precious liquid has consequently become a valuable commodity that is often imported from other planets.

The Lars homestead near Mos Eisley is a typical moisture farm. A number of remote and distantly spaced vaporators are monitored from a modest collection of small, semi-buried rooms clustered around a central courtyard. The courtyard is also connected to a workshop and

speeder garages. The moisture farmer leads a lonely and dangerous lifestyle, constantly wary of the threats posed by marauding Tusken Raiders and scavenging Jawas.

The wildlife of Tatooine includes a number of creatures that thrive in the arid climate. Banthas are large, thick-furred quadrupeds. The males of the species have long spiralling horns that protrude from their foreheads. Banthas are found all over the galaxy, but are especially

WATTO

This slovenly and abrasive Toydarian learned to haggle from Jawas and subsequently established a relatively small shop in the busy trading district of Mos Espa Way.

Watto won Shmi and Anakin in a Podracing wager with Gardulla the Hutt, but lost Anakin – and many credits – in a wager with Jedi Master Qui-Gon Jinn.

Watto continues to trade, although he no longer owns any slaves. He is quite surprised to meet a grown-up Anakin.

TUSKEN RAIDERS

It is not known if these primitive and secretive nomads are indigenous to Tatooine, but there is no evidence that they can be found anywhere else in the galaxy.

When these creatures formerly known as Sand People destroyed Fort Tusken – a settlement established by some of Tatooine's earliest colonists – they earned the name 'Tusken Raiders' and a terrifying reputation for ruthless and indiscriminate slaughter.

Tusken Raiders roam the desert, jealously guarding their supplies of underground water and mercilessly defending intrusions into their territory. They have no permanent shelters, but establish makeshift encampments where they prolong the agony of their tortured captives.

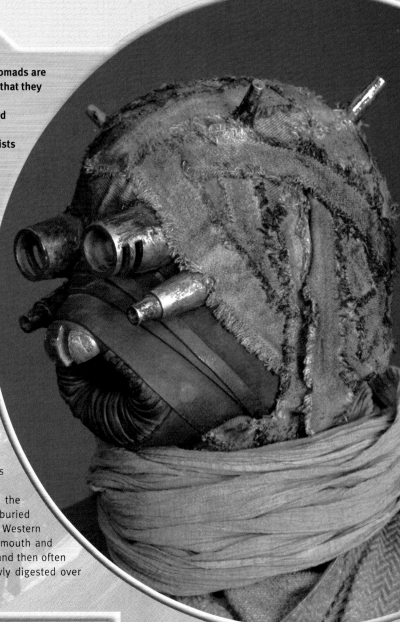

prolific on Tatooine where they are used as beasts of burden by moisture farmers and loyal pack animals by Raiders. The priests of Tatooine's Dim-U religion preach that these shambling beasts hold a secret of universal importance that is waiting to be revealed.

Krayt Dragons are the largest creatures on Tatooine. They can usually be found in mountainous areas and are feared even by the Tusken Raiders, who challenge them during the rites of passage ceremony of their young.

The most unusual creature on Tatooine is the Sarlacc, a giant arthropod whose body is largely buried beneath the sand of the Great Pit of Carkoon in the Western Dune Sea. Only the Sarlacc's enormous gaping mouth and clutching tentacles are visible from the surface, and then often only by victims who are sucked inside and slowly digested over many years.

JAWAS

These diminutive, foul-smelling scavengers are unreliable thieves and swindlers who roam Tatooine aboard huge Sandcrawler vehicles. Like the Tusken Raiders, Jawas cover their bodies almost entirely as protection from the ubiquitous suns, wind, and sand. With only their orange glowing eyes visible beneath the hoods of their cloaks, Jawas appear friendly and unthreatening. They are unscrupulous tradespeople, however – many a farmer has come to regret purchasing a faulty droid from these scuttling creatures.

CORUSCANT

The heart of the Coruscant System, this planet is adjacent to the Deep Core and has been the centre of government since the earliest days of the Republic.

The seas and oceans of Coruscant have long since been drained, and the surface of the planet is now virtually smothered by one huge city. From space, Coruscant resembles a giant amber sphere studded with twinkling beacons of light. Once through the atmosphere and into the smoggy skies, the transparisteel and smoked duracrete buildings seem less romantic, and the lights give way to dank streets that remain in the shadows of taller buildings.

Fast food joints, drinking dives, and dubious nightclubs cater to the myriad alien species that jostle along the pavements. Nightclubs can be especially dangerous places where deathstick dealers can mingle in bars with bounty hunters, smugglers, kidnappers, and other miscreants.

IMPERIAL CENTRE

In the years following the Clone Wars, Emperor Palpatine adopts Coruscant as his seat of power and renames the planet 'Imperial Centre'. Following the success of the rebellion and the Emperor's demise, great celebrations take place as the people of Coruscant reclaim their planet from Imperial rule.

This teeming megalopolis is home to over a trillion inhabitants, and space is of such a premium that architects have no choice but to design taller and taller skyscrapers. Some of the tallest buildings are over a kilometre high and extend to the lower reaches of the atmosphere.

With the exception of air taxis, all traffic is confined to auto-navigating skylanes. Deviating from those skylanes can prove dangerous, as Obi-Wan discovers when Anakin's pursuit of Zam Wesell brings their borrowed airspeeder perilously close to many mid-air collisions.

Coruscant is too far from its small white sun to have a climate that is truly comfortable for humans. Immense orbital mirrors warm the planet's upper and lower latitudes by refocusing and distributing stellar energy. The most densely populated areas of the planet are the temperate zones around the equator, but even these have a reputation for being rather cold and bleak.

The planet's natural resources are almost entirely exhausted. Supplies of ice from what remains of Coruscant's polar ice caps are

transported around the planet to meet the demand for water, and giant starfreighters bring food and raw materials from other worlds. It is on one such freighter that Anakin, Padmé, and R2-D2 make their secret journey from Coruscant to the relative safety of Naboo.

The chaotic landscape features edifices of considerable architectural beauty. It is within such buildings that Coruscant earns its reputation as the galactic centre of government and peacekeeping.

The Galactic Senate meets in a huge domed building that emerges mushroom-like from the urban sprawl of Coruscant. The Senate Chamber includes 1024 platforms used by Senators, diplomats, and other representatives. When any such dignitary wishes to make a speech – such as during the debate on whether to create a grand army of the Republic – their platform detaches and floats into the middle of the cavernous rotunda. Cam Droids hover before them, relaying their speeches to curious onlookers.

Since the end of her second and final term of office, Queen Padmé Amidala has become a Senator representing Naboo. She believes passionately in the democratic process, and is determined to participate in Senate debates despite whatever obstacles are put in her path. The most powerful member of the Senate is Supreme Chancellor Palpatine, a beleaguered man who strives to uphold the values of the Republic in the face of corrupt Senators and aggressive Separatists. Palpatine is a very private individual, who often withdraws to his quarters. The strange scarlet décor of his apartment matches the robes of his imposing guards.

The Jedi Knights are the Republic's peacekeepers, and they are also based on Coruscant. The Jedi Temple is a flat, square building amid an unusually barren area of land. The Temple is crowned by five towering spires – one in each corner and a larger central spire that dominates them all. The circular, glass-walled Jedi Council Chamber overlooks Coruscant from the top of one of the smaller spires. Within the chamber, Masters Yoda and Mace Windu chair meetings with ten other representatives of the noble order. On the nearby training veranda, prospective Jedi are tutored in the ways of the Force.

Another of the smaller spires houses the Jedi Archives, which are the computer-encoded repository of the Order's immense knowledge. The analysis room contains row after row of glass cubicles, in which objects can be identified by SP-4 Droids. The Archives Library is an awe-inspiring mixture of ancient and modern. Finely chiselled effigies of renowned Jedi Knights stand before banks of illuminated computer panels that stretch into the distance. Archivists such as Madame Jocasta Nu are able to draw upon their memories and experiences of such venerated Jedi as Count Dooku, but are just as adept at initiating gravitational scans, star-map holograms, and the other state-of-the-art facilities the library offers.

The Jedi Knights and the Republic they serve are facing a desperate future, but Coruscant's teeming infrastructure and enviable galactic position are unlikely to be challenged. It is unthinkable that the planet should ever lose its position as 'The Jewel of the Core Worlds'.

THE JEDI HIGH COUNCIL

The Jedi Council is led by senior Jedi Masters Yoda and Mace Windu. Their fellow councillors are: Ki-Adi-Mundi, a Cerean with a high-domed head that holds a binary brain; Depa Billaba, a female Chalactan who was orphaned by space pirates; Eeth Koth, a Zabrak from the planet Iridonia; Even Piell, a diminutive warrior who lost his left eye in a battle with terrorists; Saesee Tiin, an Iktotchi telepath and pioneering test-pilot; Oppo Rancisis, a former monarch of the planet Thisspias; Plo Koon, a native of the planet Dorin who is sensitive to the oxygen-rich atmosphere of Coruscant; and Adi Gallia, an intuitive warrior born on Coruscant.

Jedi Council members Yaddle and Yareal Poof have died since the Battle of Naboo. Their places have been taken by Coleman Trebor, an amphibious Vurk from Sembla, and Shaak Ti, a Togruta from Shili.

THE WILDLIFE
OF CORUSCANT

There is little opportunity for wildlife to flourish on Coruscant, but several species have endured the planet's urban transformation.

Granite slugs occasionally make their way up from the surface, clinging to the sides of buildings. The slugs often fall victim to hawk-bats, which ride thermals from the bowels of the city and swoop on their unsuspecting prey. The hawk-bats are tolerated not only because they offer economical pest-control, but also because their eggs are considered a delicacy.

The level roof of one skyscraper is home to the Skydome Botanical Gardens. The gardens were constructed by a philanthropist who grew wealthy following his establishment of the Galactic News Service.

The only place on Coruscant to see many of the planet's vanished species is the Holographic Zoo for Extinct Animals. Three-dimensional dioramas depict such creatures as the mammoth krabbex, the manticore, and the singing fig trees of Pil-Diller.

Naboo

Naboo is a lush world of swampy lakes, rolling meadows and green hills that lies close to the border of the Outer Rim territories.

The planet is most conspicuously populated by the Naboo, a peaceful and scholarly race who live above ground. The indigenous Gungans live beneath the swamps and seas in awe-inspiring colonies of hydrostatic bubbles.

The ancient underwater settlement of Otoh Gunga is the Gungans' largest city, and has seen impressive expansion under the energetic leadership of Boss Nass. The Gungans traverse the planet in Bongo submersibles, risking attack from the fearsome sea beasts that dwell within its watery core. The conflict with the Trade Federation marked the beginning of a new era of co-operation between the Gungans and the Naboo. In the interests of preserving ecological stability and alleviating overcrowding in Otoh Gunga, the two races launched an ambitious joint venture to colonise Ohma-D'un, one of Naboo's three moons.

The capital of Naboo is Theed, a city of classical architecture and tranquil beauty. Theed is situated near the Virdugo Plunge, a waterfall

fed by the river Solleu. The city is known for its grand libraries, museums, theatres and other cultural buildings. Padmé Amidala's father Ruwee teaches at the local university, and the family make their modest home in a side street of Theed's residential area. Padmé's parents feel that their daughter has already given Naboo enough of her time and energy, and that she should bring her diplomatic career to an end.

Points of interest in Theed include the Hall of Perri-Teeka, an impressive monument to a revered statesman; Broadbery Meadow, a secluded garden reachable only by boat; the banqueting rotunda built by the Earl of Vis, a cousin of the old king; Guido's Tower, one of the oldest structures in the city; and the Parnelli Museum of Art.

The Royal Palace is the largest building in the city, and is where the elected monarch convenes with his or her Royal Advisory Council. During the reign of Queen Amidala, the council included the Education Regent Lufta Shif, Chief Architect Hugo Eckener, Music Advisor Hela Brandes, and Master of Sciences Graf Zapalo. Only the governor of Naboo and the head of security hold permanent office. Governor Sio Bibble was elected during the reign of King Veruna and continues to serve under Queen Jamillia. Captain Panaka was appointed head of

Padmé and Anakin begin an idyllic stay, wandering through the rolling meadows and enjoying the privacy of a lodge in the middle of a translucent lake. Padmé last visited the area when she was a schoolgirl, in a time before the heavy burden of political duty dominated her life. Ultimately, Anakin is so overwhelmed by his feelings for Padmé that he relinquishes his internal struggle with the Jedi code of honour and kisses her.

Swept away by the romance of the situation and inspired by some of the most breathtaking scenery on a beautiful planet, Anakin and Padmé embark on a path that will have momentous consequences for them both – and the galaxy.

security following the death of the old king and played a crucial role during the Battle of Naboo, even though his Palace Guard was outnumbered and under-equipped to face the technological might of the Trade Federation. Panaka now guards Queen Jamillia, while Senator Amidala is protected by Panaka's cousin, Captain Typho.

Anakin and Padmé share sentimental memories of Naboo. On the couple's return to Theed, Anakin tells Padmé he has thought about the city every day since his last visit ten years before. He fondly recalls the way the palace shimmers in the sunlight, and the sweet scent of flowers on the breeze.

Padmé recalls her childhood memories of the soft sound of distant waterfalls. 'The first time I saw the capital, I was very young,' she tells Anakin. 'I'd never seen a waterfall before. I thought they were so beautiful... I never dreamed one day I'd live in the palace.'

But for all Theed's beauty, it remains too conspicuous a destination for a young woman who has narrowly escaped two assassination attempts. Padmé and Anakin head for the safety of Naboo's Lake Country, which boasts some of the most isolated – and picturesque – locations on the planet.

JAR JAR BINKS

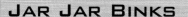

The ebullient Jar Jar Binks has come a long way since he was exiled from Otoh Gunga by Boss Nass. Jar Jar returned to the city in an outrageous contravention of the 'nocombackie' law, but went on to win Boss Nass's respect when he became an unwitting hero of the Battle of Naboo. Binks has relocated to Coruscant and acts as a representative of his home planet in the Galactic Senate. He is overjoyed at being reunited with Obi-Wan and Anakin when they are first assigned to protect Amidala. When the lovesick Anakin frets that Amidala doesn't think of him in the same way he regards her, Jar Jar is on hand to offer some reassuring words.

When Padmé is forced to leave Coruscant for the refuge of Naboo, she appoints Jar Jar to act on her behalf in the forthcoming debate on the Military Creation Act. Jar Jar is a well-meaning soul who speaks with what he considers to be the best intentions. But is Amidala wise to trust his judgement on such a crucial issue?

KAMINO

Beyond the Outer Rim, approximately 12 parsecs outside the Rishi Maze, lies a planet that doesn't exist – at least in the Jedi Archives.

The toxic saberdart that kills bounty hunter Zam Wesell originates from Kamino, but Obi-Wan's efforts to establish the location of the planet in the Jedi Archives prove fruitless. Madame Jocasta Nu tells him that if Kamino does not appear in the Jedi records then it does not exist. But a star-map hologram reveals an incriminating area of gravitational pull without a planet at its centre. The Jedi Archives have been tampered with, and the records of Kamino have clearly been erased.

Obi-Wan travels towards the location of the gravitational pull and discovers a radiant dark-blue world. The last ice age on Kamino covered half the planet in continental glaciers, which melted over thousands of years. As the sea level on the planet swelled, land-based species died out and the Kaminoans were forced to build their settlements on higher and higher ground. Eventually, there wasn't any ground left.

Obi-Wan arrives at a landing platform in the capital Tipoca, the largest city on Kamino. Tipoca is a typical Kaminoan settlement, built on giant stilts that are constantly buffeted by the waves of an endless ocean. As with many other Kaminoan cities, the stilts that support Tipoca are built atop a former high plateau now submerged in some of the planet's most shallow water.

When Obi-Wan arrives, the rain lashes the landing platform and the wind howls around his ears. The Kaminoan climate is not always so stormy, but during the period known as 'the beautiful season' such inhospitable weather is common.

The Kaminoans are a race that evolved for survival both in and out of the water that bordered the little remaining land on their planet. That ground has disappeared, but the Kaminoans remain air-breathing land animals partly adapted for water. Kaminoans have elongated bones in their long, thin necks. The males of the species sport distinctive crests on the tops of their heads.

'These Kaminoans keep to themselves,' Dexter Jettster tells his old friend Obi-Wan. 'They're cloners, damned good ones too.' Kaminoans speak in soft, sonorous tones that make their amoral attitude towards eugenics and their thriving cloning business seem all the more surprising.

The functional aesthetic of Kaminoan cities has got nothing to do with a lack of materials (the planet has abundant resources below its sea bed) but more to do with the way the Kaminoans' outlook has been affected by their long struggle against sea monsters and their own planet's changing, harsh climate. They have developed a sustaining inner philosophy, and have cultivated a sort of austere beauty as exhibited by the external elegance of their stilt-suspended settlements. The cities are a rare and impressive highlight in a watery landscape.

The Kaminoans' inward-thinking culture has isolated them from the affairs of the galaxy, and they are not even members of the Republic. When a Jedi Master called Sifo-Dyas placed an order for a clone army the Kaminoans had no reason to suspect that his request wasn't supported by the Jedi Council. Kaminoan Prime Minister Lama Su knows little of the Jedi Council and the Galactic Senate, and cares less

about any internal struggles on Coruscant. He works for the highest bidder, and ensures that his people cultivate an army with the care and diligence that clients have come to expect.

The model for the clones in the army was bounty hunter Jango Fett, whom Obi-Wan deduces was responsible for the death of assassin Zam Wesell – and ultimately responsible for the attempts on Senator Amidala's life. Jango's arrangement with the Kaminoans allows for accommodation in Tipoca and a perfect clone he can call his son. Boba is not subjected to the growth acceleration or genetic manipulation that has turned the army of cloned embryos into fully grown – and fully obedient – men. Boba is a ten-year-old boy, but he has already learned much from his father.

The isolated Kaminoans continued working on the clone army for ten years following the original commission, even though they heard nothing from Master Sifo-Dyas or anyone else on the Jedi Council. When Obi-Wan arrives at Tipoca City he is met by Taun We and taken to see Kaminoan Prime Minister Lama Su. The Kaminoans believe that Obi-Wan has come to check on the progress they have made

Aiwhas

Many Kaminoans choose to ride giant aiwha birds when they need to make undersea and airborne journeys. Like the Kaminoans, aiwhas can breathe above and below sea level. They break the surface of the Kaminoan sea and take to the skies, leaving a trail of cascading sea-water in their wake. Powerful pectoral muscles beat smooth, waterproof wings, while Kaminoan passengers keep a firm grip on reins attached to the creatures' necks. Aiwhas use their natural sonar abilities for navigating underwater, and emit a high-pitched whistling noise when airborne.

over the last ten years, and Lama Su proudly reports that they are on schedule: Two hundred thousand units are ready, with another million on the way.

Obi-Wan reveals that Sifo-Dyas was killed ten years ago, although he plays along with the idea that the clone army was indeed commissioned by the Jedi on the Republic's behalf. It is debatable how much the Kaminoans would care, even if they doubted the veracity of the order.

GEONOSIS

Nothing is as it seems on Geonosis – a close inspection of the planet's seemingly mundane features is rewarded with some disturbing revelations.

This red planet lies in the Outer Rim, a mere parsec away from neighbouring Tatooine. When approached from space, Geonosis appears an unspoilt world surrounded by two rings in close proximity to each other. It is only when the traveller approaches the rings that they are revealed to comprise two different strands of the same asteroid belt.

The asteroids in Geonosis's rings provide valuable cover for Obi-Wan Kenobi's Delta-7 starfighter when he pursues Jango Fett's *Slave I* from Kamino. Some of the giant orbiting rocks are big enough to hide a spaceship – Jango Fett skilfully pilots *Slave I* through a narrow passage in one of the larger asteroids and Obi-Wan attaches his ship to a blasted-out area on the pitted side of another.

Although they appear slender from a distance, the asteroid rings of Geonosis are deep and broad enough to conceal more than just a pair of skirmishing starfighters. A huge fleet of Trade Federation battleships lurks among the rocks and other orbiting debris that offer valuable cover from scanner detection.

The relatively featureless surface of Geonosis affords Obi-Wan little opportunity for cover when he first arrives, but he finds an overhanging rock under which to leave his ship before he explores. The night can be a dangerous time on Geonosis – large insectoid predators and aggressive snakes roam the craggy landscape, and the howls of strange animals fill the air.

The arid plains of the planet are scarred from years of cosmic ray bombardment, and the flat horizon is only occasionally punctuated by buttes, mesa, and towering rock formations. Once again, however, all is not what it seems. The clusters of rock formations on Geonosis are not a natural phenomena, but buildings that form the tips of cities that extend for tens of thousands of square feet beneath the ground.

Geonosians are a physically intimidating race conditioned to live and work in caste-segregated hives. The vast majority of Geonosians are subservient to the ruling caste, and throughout Geonosian society, there is evidence of a biologically engineered class system. Some Geonosians have wings, while drones do not; some Geonosians threaten Obi-Wan with sonic blasters, while others carry spears.

The blind obedience of menial Geonosians makes them an easily exploitable workforce for the upper classes, who have built a highly profitable business manufacturing Battle Droids, Super Battle Droids, and Droideka Droids for the Trade Federation and its allies. Spiralling conveyor belts carry components deep into the bowels of the planet. The process is maintained by drone Geonosians on the ground and monitored by winged Geonosians who watch from alcoves in the vaulted ceilings of the cathedral-like structures. They squat like gargoyles, waiting to swoop on intruders.

If there is one thing that unites Geonosians of all classes, it is their xenophobia. A traditionally isolationist species, they fear espionage attempts by rivals eager to learn the secrets behind their latest droids.

BATTLE DROIDS

The Republic and its Jedi peacekeepers maintain an era of relative stability, and there is little need for armies of sentient beings. Like a number of other organisations, the Trade Federation commission Battle Droids and droidekas ostensibly for defensive purposes. Ten years ago, however, the Galactic Senate was unaware that the Trade Federation was actually amassing a huge droid army to launch an invasion of Naboo.

The Battle of Naboo revealed a fatal flaw in the design of the skeletal droids – they were all co-ordinated by a central computer in an orbiting control ship. When Anakin Skywalker destroyed the ship, the thousands of droids on the planet's surface were rendered useless.

The Senate has since prohibited the use of droid forces, but Poggle the Lesser has secretly constructed what he calls 'the finest army in the galaxy' for his Trade Federation client Nute Gunray and his associates. The foundries on Geonosis continue to supply Battle Droids – and now manufacture a Super Battle Droid, a strengthened model capable of independent function.

Captured prisoners join convicted Geonosian criminals in the open-air execution arena. The vast coliseum, which is carved out of solid rock, is part of a loose circuit of gladiatorial venues which thrive despite the disapproval of the Republic. The games provide entertainment for lower-class Geonosians, and an amusement for the ruling classes who sometimes stage contests to impress each other for political reasons. For unusually intelligent Geonosians unlucky enough to be born into the lower castes, participating in the games provides the only chance they will ever get to escape the misery of their downtrodden lifestyles and the rigid social expectations of the upper classes. Triumph in the arena is often a hollow victory, however – while lower- and middle-class Geonosians may win the right to talk to their superiors, they can never earn their respect.

Poggle the Lesser, the corrupt Archduke of Geonosis, presides over two major types of combat from the most expensive seat in the house: battles against wild beasts – such as the reek, nexu, and acklay – and death-matches where sentient beings do battle with one another.

The execution arena on Geonosis becomes the venue for the biggest battle it has ever seen when the Republic's clone army descends on the droids of the Separatists. Later, in a secret hangar elsewhere on Geonosis, the Jedi fight Count Dooku in a lightsaber duel that will decide the fate of the entire Republic....

DROIDEKAS

Droidekas, or 'Destroyer' Droids, are manufactured in the same foundries that create Battle Droids. These rapid deployment machines literally roll into the heart of the action and unfurl their weaponry with devastating effect. Droidekas are protected by bronzium armour shells and starfighter-class shields. Few opponents can withstand the firepower of their twin double-barrelled heavy-repeating blasters.

Droidekas were originally designed by the Colicoids of Colla IV, and fashioned in the image of their insect-like creators. Droidekas were used by the Trade Federation in the Battle of Naboo and are included in the forces being rallied against the Republic by Count Dooku.

The Making of Episode II

FILMING

STAR WARS: Episode I – *The Phantom Menace*, the long-awaited resumption of the world's favourite film trilogy, opened in American cinemas on 19 May 1999. Over the coming weeks and months, audiences flocked to see the first film George Lucas had directed in over 20 years.

Although it was the fourth *Star Wars* film, Episode I described the events at the beginning of the saga Lucas first devised in 1973. 'I just sat down and went through the entire story,' he recalls. 'I wrote a treatment or a book of notes that went through all the scripts... It was reasonably loose, but it laid out the basic story of what happens, who does what to whom, and the various major issues. And that's how it came about that there was enough material for six scripts.'

The trilogy of prequels that precede the events of *Star Wars*: Episode IV – *A New Hope* (released in 1977) centre on the character Anakin Skywalker and the events that transform him into the cruel Sith Lord – Darth Vader. The stories that are unfolding in these three films have taken over 25 years to appear. The time taken to produce each film is similarly unusual. 'Episode I actually took us five years,' says prequel trilogy producer Rick McCallum, 'including one serious year of massive conceptual art design which affected not only Episode I but also Episode II and even III to a certain degree. They're very complicated to make. It takes 18 months just to do the effects, and it takes six months to prepare for those effects, so that's two years right there. It takes us basically seven months to prepare and four months to shoot... that's another year. And then it takes us a year to conceptualise and have everything together to make the necessary commitments for locations. We don't just shoot in the studio, we stop in five different countries, we have to get permissions, schedule, just mammoth things.'

Clockwise from top left: Producer Rick McCallum, 'A'-camera focus puller Brett Matthews and Director George Lucas at Fox Studios in Sydney; Lucas and director of photography David Tattersall (wearing cap) on location in Tunisia; Lucas at Villa Balbianello, Lake Como, Italy; The crew shelter the cameras from the rain at Villa Balbianello; Lucas and assistant director James McTeigue in Tozeur, Tunisia.

Lucas began work on his script for Episode II in September 1999, and knew enough about its major requirements to brief his department heads at the end of the year. 'George would gradually give us information from December onwards in terms of things that we needed to do, and sets that he was sure were going to be needed,' says Episode II production designer Gavin Bocquet. 'And there was only one that we actually really built, or got near to finishing, that he later decided probably wasn't in any more because he had combined those two scenes into one environment.'

Informal location scouting for Episode II began in Europe mere days after *The Phantom Menace* opened. Over the subsequent months, Lucas, McCallum and Bocquet visited numerous potential locations. It was decided to establish the base of operations for the new movie in Australia. The previous *Star Wars* movies had all been shot in England, and the relocation to Sydney's Fox Studios represented a significant departure.

The most radical innovation introduced on the new film was yet to come, however. Following four months of systematic testing with the 24-P high definition digital camera – the result of a collaboration between Sony and Panavision – Lucas felt confident enough to shoot Episode II without using film. The 'P' stands for 'Progressive Scan', which means the camera records 24 frames per second – the same number as a traditional film camera. 'The tests have convinced me that the familiar look and feel of motion picture film are fully present,' said

Lucas in April 2000. 'The quality of the two is indistinguishable on the large screen. It's an exciting step that we are taking, and, working with Sony and Panavision, we plan to further advance the system over the coming years. *Star Wars*: Episode II is our first giant step.'

Confirmation of this widely anticipated move caused something of a sensation in the film industry, and enormous speculation built over the results and implications for future productions. 'There is so much fear being projected all over by cameramen and studios,' said McCallum following the announcement. 'As far as we're concerned, we're not trying to convince the world that they need to go a different way in making movies. It's the way *we* want to go. We're not trying to change their minds. If people like film, fine, let them shoot on film. For us, film is not as practical, because every single shot we do has a digital effect in it. There is no point in us shooting on film. It is just much easier and more economical – and the results are fabulous.'

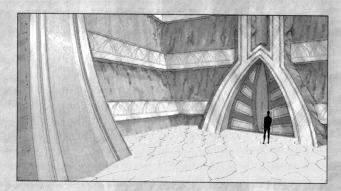

Clockwise from above: Production art depicting a secret cavern on Geonosis; George Lucas at Villa Balbianello; Natalie Portman and Hayden Christensen at Chott El Jerrid, Tunisia, with photographer Lisa Tomasetti; Lucas with Brett Matthews and 'A'-camera/Steadicam operator Brad Shield at Fox Studios; A panorama of reference photographs from the location reconnaissance at Lake Como.

Casting director Robin Gurland began work on Episode II in November 1999. A number of familiar faces returned from Episode I, including Ewan McGregor as Obi-Wan Kenobi, Natalie Portman as Padmé Amidala and Samuel L Jackson as Mace Windu. Notable additions to the *Star Wars* universe include Jimmy Smits as Senator Bail Organa and Christopher Lee as Count Dooku.

Many of the movie's smaller roles were filled by Australian actors. Gurland received submissions from such disparate locations as Perth and Sydney. She attended the Sydney Film Festival, and recruited two cast-members after excursions to local theatre productions. Some of the Australian actors were cast as younger versions of characters last seen in Episode IV – Joel Edgerton was chosen to play a young Owen Lars (previously played by Phil Brown) and Bonnie Piesse was chosen to play Beru Whitesun (previously played by Shelagh Fraser).

'I was certainly looking for a physical match as well as someone who could act,' says Gurland, describing the casting of Joel Edgerton. 'Joel's parents have to take the credit for the former, not me – but boy was I lucky! It's frightening how close they are in appearance. And he's such a strong actor, so that's the real plus... [It was the] same with Beru. I went to Melbourne and I met Bonnie Piesse, and again there was such a lovely match there, and she was the right age, and she was a very strong actor, so it was perfect.'

Other local talent included Leeanna Walsmann, who was cast as ill-fated bounty hunter Zam Wesell. New Zealanders Temuera Morrison and Daniel Logan played Jango Fett and his clone son, Boba, respectively.

The most difficult role to fill was that of the film's teenage lead, Anakin Skywalker. The nine-year-old Anakin was played by the eight-year-old Jake Lloyd in Episode I, but the script for the new movie was set ten years on, so an older actor had to be found. Gurland received 1500 submissions and watched over 400 videotaped tests before submitting a list of 30 contenders for Lucas's approval. She admits to being close to the end of her tether before she met Hayden Christensen. 'It sounds very corny,' she says, 'but this is the truth: He came in and initially there was this physical thing... He is one of the strongest actors I've come across in a long, long time.' Hayden's casting was officially announced at the beginning of May 2000, the month before filming was due to begin.

Clockwise from above: Natalie Portman and Hayden Christensen's first day on set at Fox Studios included this discussion with George Lucas; Bonnie Piesse and Joel Edgerton were cast as younger versions of Beru and Owen, two characters first seen in Episode IV; Natalie Portman and Hayden Christensen on location in Matmata, Tunisia; George Lucas with casting director Robin Gurland and actor Temuera Morrison at Fox Studios; Natalie Portman and Hayden Christensen pictured during their first day on set at Fox Studios.

Gavin Bocquet and his team continued work in Sydney during the busy prelude to filming. Fox Studios' 20,000 square foot construction workshop housed 250 metal workers, carpenters, painters, and other craftspeople working three shifts a day, seven days a week. 'There is a much bigger emphasis on the art department than on other projects, and less of the huge actors' entourages that other projects might have,' said production supervisor Stephen Jones. 'People in our film won't be surrounding themselves with the periphery of staff that many films have. The sets and the quality of the costuming and art department are of a very high standard, and it is clear to me that the money goes on the screen.'

Bocquet and his team designed and constructed 67 sets. This was 13 more than had been required for Episode I. 'George had always told us that Episode II would be smaller, at least visually,' says Bocquet. 'I can say now that it's not! I mean the story, on the one hand, is quite intimate, in terms of relationships and things. So that side of it is smaller. But as far as the visual scope of it, in terms of the number of environments, the type of environments, and the speed that we move through them, it's actually harder for us.'

The most up-to-the wire element in the whole pre-production process proved to be the shooting script. During May and June, Lucas worked with British scriptwriter Jonathan Hales on the final drafts, the last of which was delivered to the crew just three days before filming began.

Rick McCallum raised his clapperboard for the first morning of principal photography on 26 June 2000 – three years to the day after shooting started on Episode I. Three months of filming and 18 months of post-production lay ahead, but the man with the ultimate responsibility for it all never lost his sense of humour. 'It's hard for me to remember if I'm still shooting Episode I, the Special Edition, the [Episode I] DVD, or Episode II!' joked Lucas.

Filming took place on all six stages at Fox Studios and in surrounding warehouses. 'I'd never been to Australia before,' says actor Ian McDiarmid, who returned to the role of Palpatine. 'It was a big difference from being down the road in London, but *Star Wars* and Australia go together very well. Like everyone else, I didn't know the Australian crew, and they of course didn't know George because he had not long arrived. So they didn't really know what to expect, and they were, as usual, thinking, "Oh my God, it's *Star Wars*," as everybody does.'

Above: The sets come together at Fox Studios.
Below: The set of the Outlander gambling club at Fox Studios.
Opposite: Rick McCallum raises the clapperboard on 26 June 2000 – the first day of principal photography at Fox Studios.

FOX STUDIOS

The logo of Sydney's Fox Studios invites visitors to, 'just imagine', and there can be few better aids to the imagination than the world's newest major studio development.

The 60-acre site was opened by Twentieth Century Fox's parent company News Corporation in May 1998, and has since hosted such major successes as *The Matrix, Mission: Impossible 2* and *Moulin Rouge*.

The studio complex is minutes from Sydney's city centre and airport, and is only a short distance from such diverse locations as bushland, mountains, and surf-fringed beaches.

Five of the six soundstages are purpose-built, although Stage 1 is a converted heritage pavilion with distinctive red-brick walls. Lucasfilm occupied all six stages during the production of Episode II, and drew huge black blinds across the windows of the two stages that are overlooked by tourists visiting the now partially-shuttered Fox Studio Tour. 'We control everything the minute you go through those gates,' said Rick McCallum. 'We have taken over areas that they never even thought could be stages.'

Filming progressed smoothly, and Lucas took time to praise the Sony/Panavision camera. 'A lot of the digital thing is technical,' he said. 'It's the difference between sketching with a quill pen and sketching with a nice felt tip. They're just two different technologies. And in a lot of cases, one is easier to work with. And with one you have to be really careful and slower, and the other one is more fluid and you can think faster. So it's really not as dramatic as the introduction of sound was, or colour in terms of the image and what you can get from it.'

McCallum kept a careful eye on the schedule, while Lucas completed an impressive average of 36 set-ups per day. Location filming began at the end of August. With all the precision of a military manoeuvre, the crew visited Lake Como in Italy (the location for Anakin and Amidala's romantic stay in the Naboo Lake Country lodge); the Plaza d'Espana in Seville, Spain (outside on the palace grounds); and spent one week in Tunisia, the traditional setting for the planet Tatooine in the *Star Wars* films.

At one time, shooting locations after studio work would have been considered unusual. 'Those days are long gone,' explains McCallum. 'The reason that you used to have to do your exteriors first was so that you knew what your lighting conditions would be like for the interiors. In the digital world, it doesn't matter. We can change the exterior to anything we want, to match the interior. So you deal with what you want instead of what you get. Then what you want, you re-create. Even if it's a rainy day, it doesn't matter.'

At the end of the schedule, in September 2000, a handful of scenes were shot at Elstree Studios in Borehamwood, north of London. This was a surprise return to the studio that had hosted the filming for Episodes IV to VI and the *Indiana Jones* trilogy. The present-day Elstree is a shadow of its former self – many of the sound stages that Lucasfilm used in the late 1970s and 1980s have sadly been demolished – but McCallum nevertheless praised the unique talent that necessitated Lucasfilm's return. And many others quoted the oft-repeated belief that the studio had been a 'lucky charm' for Lucas in the past.

Top: A location reconnaissance photograph showing Villa Balbianello at Lake Como, Italy.
Above: George Lucas meets Star Wars *fans on location at Plaza d'Espana, Seville, Spain.*
Opposite: Samuel L Jackson confers with George Lucas during the filming of the execution arena scenes at Fox Studios.
Below: Rick McCallum, visual effects supervisor John Knoll, George Lucas and Natalie Portman relax between takes at Ealing Studios.

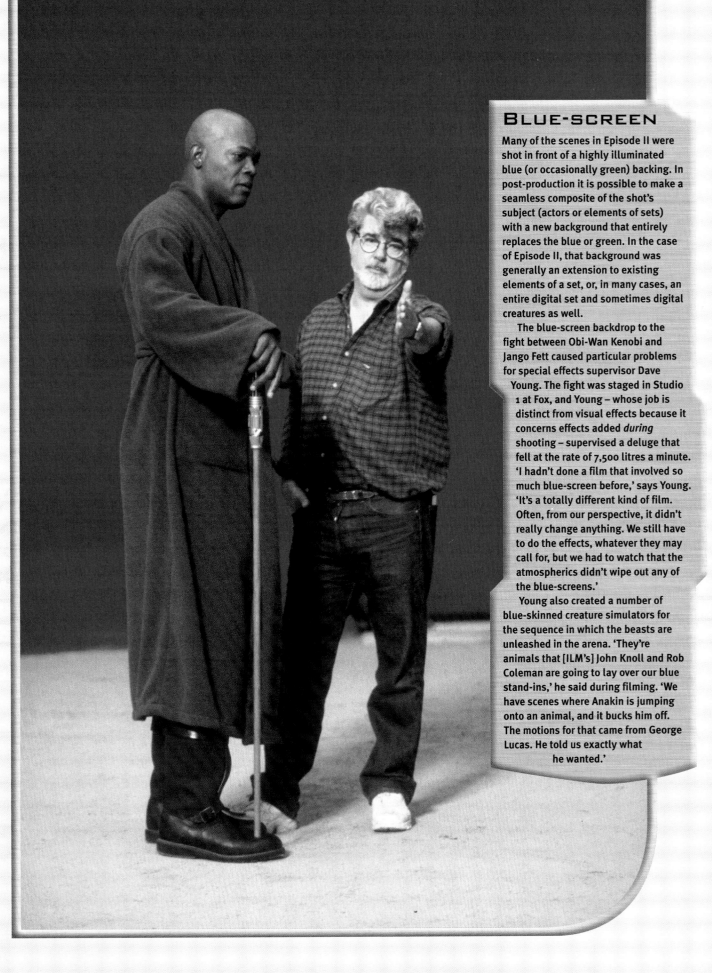

BLUE-SCREEN

Many of the scenes in Episode II were shot in front of a highly illuminated blue (or occasionally green) backing. In post-production it is possible to make a seamless composite of the shot's subject (actors or elements of sets) with a new background that entirely replaces the blue or green. In the case of Episode II, that background was generally an extension to existing elements of a set, or, in many cases, an entire digital set and sometimes digital creatures as well.

The blue-screen backdrop to the fight between Obi-Wan Kenobi and Jango Fett caused particular problems for special effects supervisor Dave Young. The fight was staged in Studio 1 at Fox, and Young – whose job is distinct from visual effects because it concerns effects added *during* shooting – supervised a deluge that fell at the rate of 7,500 litres a minute. 'I hadn't done a film that involved so much blue-screen before,' says Young. 'It's a totally different kind of film. Often, from our perspective, it didn't really change anything. We still have to do the effects, whatever they may call for, but we had to watch that the atmospherics didn't wipe out any of the blue-screens.'

Young also created a number of blue-skinned creature simulators for the sequence in which the beasts are unleashed in the arena. 'They're animals that [ILM's] John Knoll and Rob Coleman are going to lay over our blue stand-ins,' he said during filming. 'We have scenes where Anakin is jumping onto an animal, and it bucks him off. The motions for that came from George Lucas. He told us exactly what he wanted.'

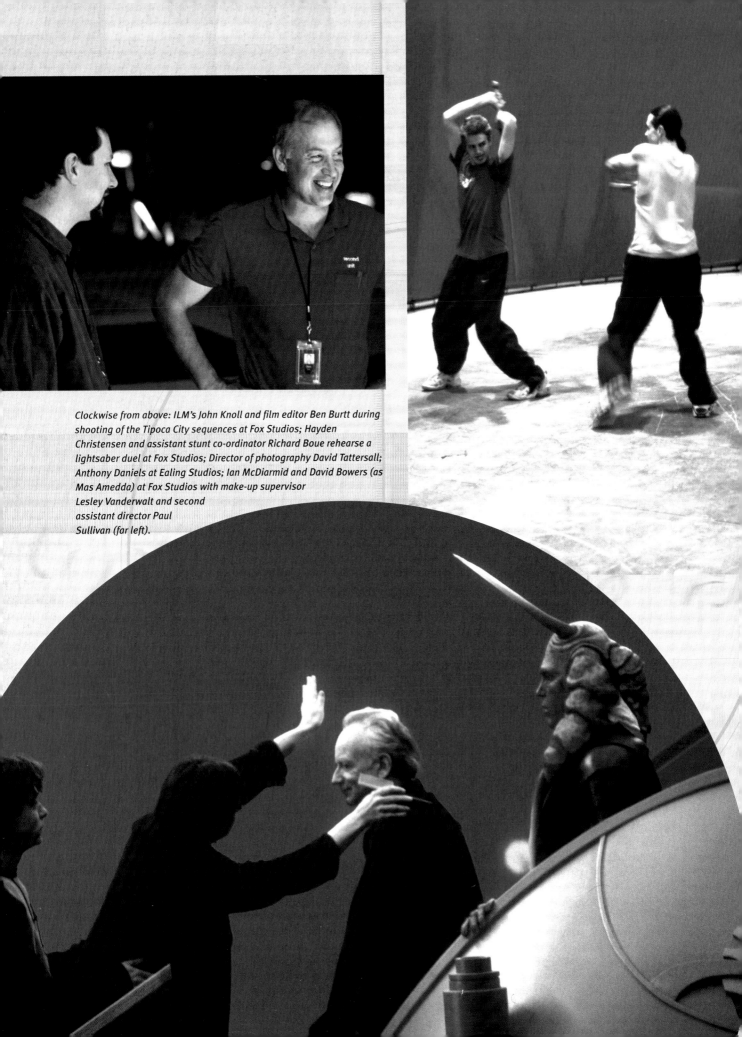

Clockwise from above: ILM's John Knoll and film editor Ben Burtt during shooting of the Tipoca City sequences at Fox Studios; Hayden Christensen and assistant stunt co-ordinator Richard Boue rehearse a lightsaber duel at Fox Studios; Director of photography David Tattersall; Anthony Daniels at Ealing Studios; Ian McDiarmid and David Bowers (as Mas Amedda) at Fox Studios with make-up supervisor Lesley Vanderwalt and second assistant director Paul Sullivan (far left).

After 61 days shooting in five countries, in conditions ranging from torrential rain to searing desert heat, principal photography came to an end later that month. The making of Episode II was, however, far from over. Sets were struck and the crew disbanded, as the centre of operations shifted to Marin County in California. Industrial Light & Magic, the legendary visual effects division of Lucas Digital, picked up where the camera crew left off, and the long process of post-production began.

Working in parallel with ILM, Lucas and his film editor Ben Burtt began assembling a rough cut of the film at Lucasfilm's headquarters, Skywalker Ranch. That rough cut ran to approximately two-and-a-half hours (approximately half the length of the rough cut of Episode I) and was completed in early 2001. It gave Lucas enough added insight into the ultimate structure of the film for him to plan the first phase of additional shooting.

Between 24 March and 8 April, pick-up shots and other additional filming was undertaken at West London's Ealing Studios, once the home of the legendary comedies that made Sir Alec Guinness – the original Obi-Wan Kenobi – an international star. Hayden Christensen, Samuel L Jackson, Christopher Lee, Ewan McGregor, Natalie Portman, and Anthony Daniels resumed their roles, and were joined by Oliver Ford Davis as Sio Bibble, a character he had last played in Episode I.

'It's been, all-in-all, deeply confusing,' Daniels said during filming at Ealing. 'I've walked so many miles down so many corridors and strange environments. Also, I'm confused as to where I am in the movie. Occasionally, I'll shout at George, asking where we are going, and he says, "See the movie." I said to him yesterday that I was going to have to go to the movie just to figure out what I was doing.'

Although the conditions were perhaps not as comfortable as they had been in Australia, one thing the sets at Ealing had in common with those at Fox Studios was a proliferation of blue-screen backings, in anticipation of the digital elements to be added by ILM. 'Blue used to be my favourite colour,' said Daniels, 'but I think I've overdosed on it.'

There was further shooting to come, all of which was conducted while ILM continued to add to the Episode II tapestry with breathtaking model work (which, like the studio work, was filmed digitally) and computer-generated effects. Lucas and Ben Burtt continued preparing cut after cut of the movie (McCallum predicted there would probably be five altogether) and, towards the end of 2001, some of the actors were recalled for dialogue replacement sessions at various studios.

Composer John Williams recorded his score at London's Abbey Road Studios in January 2002, and, when it was complete, the music joined the myriad elements converging to comprise the final cut of *Star Wars*: Episode II – *Attack of the Clones*.

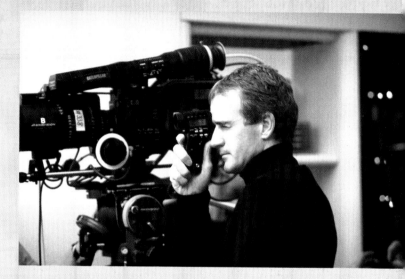

EALING STUDIOS

Construction of Ealing Studios, a West London complex that featured Britain's first purpose-built sound stage, was completed in 1931.

The studios, and the production company named after them, were home to the morale-boosting George Formby comedies of the 1930s and 40s, but are perhaps best known for the 'Ealing comedies' that began with *Hue and Cry* in 1947. Subsequent classics included *Kind Hearts and Coronets* (1949) and *The Man in the White Suit* (1951), both of which starred Alec Guinness.

Guinness, who played Obi-Wan Kenobi in the original *Star Wars* trilogy, passed away in August 2000. Anthony Daniels, who worked alongside the actor in Episode IV, remembered his late colleague during the filming of additional material at Ealing in March 2001. 'In the canteen, there are pictures up of Alec,' he said. 'It's kind of nice to think that the spirit of Obi-Wan is with us.'

The studios also evoked memories of a different kind for Christopher Lee, whose last film at Ealing was *Scott of the Antarctic* in 1948. Daniels observed that not much seemed to have changed since that era. 'Being here is like being on the set of a World War II movie,' he joked, 'The food hasn't changed much since World War II, unfortunately.'

SKYWALKER RANCH

Much of the pre- and post-production work on *Attack of the Clones* was undertaken at Skywalker Ranch, Lucasfilm's purpose-built headquarters.

The enormous success of the *Star Wars* films enabled Lucas to relocate his production company to the Ranch, a sprawling complex in an idyllic valley north of San Francisco. Crucially, Skywalker Ranch and Lucasfilm's sister companies (which include the renowned Industrial Light & Magic and Skywalker Sound) are all located some 800 kilometres away from the traditional filmmaking centre of Los Angeles.

The facility was originally named Bulltail Ranch when construction began in 1980. Lucasfilm currently plans to expand the Ranch with another facility nearby.

The digital process ultimately benefited Lucasfilm and its distributor in its preparation of prints for theatrical release. A motion picture traditionally begins with a negative, which is then processed to become an interpositive (IP) and then an internegative (IN). It is from there that a release print is struck and sent to a cinema. 'Each time you go through another process, there's an enormous amount of degradation to the image,' says McCallum. 'Now we can go from data, skipping past the original negative and the IP stage, and go straight to an IN, and then the release print. When you normally make a film you might be able to scratch six or eight release prints, or 'show prints', off the original negative. And those are the very best, pristine prints out there. We can basically do 5,000 top quality prints now, so we're really excited about that.'

Speculation about the third and final instalment in the *Star Wars* saga began before Episode II was even released. In summer 2001 McCallum confirmed that Lucas would soon start working on a script. 'For Episode III, we're trying to start the script now and move back to about four years of total [production] time because in reality that's how much time we need.'

For all the technological advances employed in Episode II, it is the dramatic innovations that the audience most eagerly awaits. Although we can predict that the story will grow darker in the new film, we can also predict the unique frisson of excitement and the unexpected that only *Star Wars* can deliver.

Above: Samuel L Jackson and George Lucas at Fox Studios.
Below: James McTeigue and George Lucas watch as Ewan McGregor is coached by stunt co-ordinator Nick Gillard at Elstree Studios.

ELSTREE STUDIOS

Construction of Elstree Studios was completed in 1926, and the facility had already hosted around 500 movies by the time Episode IV began shooting there in March 1976.

Lucasfilm used all nine soundstages during the shooting of the original trilogy, and the enormous Stage 6 became so associated with the films that it was subsequently dubbed 'The Star Wars Stage'.

Lucasfilm production *Indiana Jones and the Last Crusade* was in residence at Elstree when the studio was threatened with closure. The new owners, the Brent Walker Organisation,

demolished or sold off 12 acres of the complex in 1988 (a supermarket currently occupies much of the site) and by the 1990s only the three smallest soundstages (7, 8 and 9) remained.

Under the aegis of Hertsmere Borough Council, Elstree Studios has enjoyed something of a comeback, and the facility has recently benefited from some new investment and expansion. The Episode II scenes shot at Elstree represented the first time Lucasfilm had shot at the studio since *The Last Crusade*, and for many crewmembers they marked an emotional homecoming for the *Star Wars* saga.

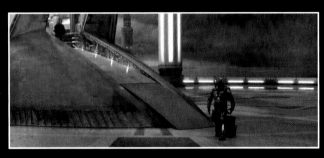

'Boba, get
on board.'

THE GAME IS UP – and Jango Fett knows it is time for him and his son, Boba, to leave Kamino. Obi-Wan Kenobi is determined to stop the bounty hunter getting away. On a rain-lashed platform in Tipoca City, Obi-Wan prepares to confront the armoured mercenary.

Obi-Wan expertly flashes his lightsaber, deflecting the blasts from Jango's weapon. Jango activates his jetpack and flies over Obi-Wan's head, landing on a nearby tower. Jango fires an explosive and Obi-Wan dives out of the way, but he soon has to contend with another opponent. From the cockpit of Jango's ship, *Slave I*, Boba aims a laser cannon at Obi-Wan.

A blast throws Obi-Wan to the ground and his lightsaber skids across the slippery surface of the wet platform. Jango grapples with Obi-Wan, and fires a restraining wire that wraps itself around Obi-Wan's wrists. Unable to reach his lightsaber and now unable to defend himself, Obi-Wan is dragged across the ground.

Obi-Wan manages to get back on his feet and tugs the wire. Jango crashes to the ground and his jetpack disengages and explodes. The Jedi rams the bounty hunter off the edge of the platform, and the two men plummet towards the rolling waves beneath. Jango halts his descent using the claws attached to his forearms; after Jango cuts the wire, Obi-Wan draws on the power of the Force and clings to a small service platform.

Obi-Wan hauls himself back on to the landing platform and retrieves his lightsaber. *Slave I* roars towards the clouds – but not before Obi-Wan attaches a discreet tracking device to its hull....

Concept Art and Production Design

CONCEPT ART and production designs are based on verbal descriptions from George Lucas or passages in his screenplay. They are refined before, during, and after principal photography, and can help many members of the crew visualise key characters, vehicles, and situations before they are created.

The following pages illustrate the diverse nature of the art department's work on *Attack of the Clones*.

Ryan Church and Erik Tiemens
Concept Design Artists

Both Ryan Church and Erik Tiemens trained in the traditional methods of painting, but there is nothing traditional about their work on *Attack of the Clones*. Church and Tiemens interact closely with the animatics department and with George Lucas, creating artwork that plays a crucial role in helping Lucas visualise his screenplay.

Church and Tiemens are concept artists who are principally charged with establishing the look, the mood, and the colour scheme of a particular scene. Their illustrations are largely concentrated on some of the most intensive CG-action parts of the film, and can provide the link between animatics and the final post-production work performed by ILM. 'We don't like to talk in terms of spaceship design or set design,' says Church. 'We prefer to talk in terms of shot design.'

Church and Tiemens joined the production in November 2000, by which time the work of Doug Chiang and many of his team-members was complete. 'We were brought on specifically for the job of providing detailed art direction, backgrounds and layouts for the stuff that had been designed by Doug's team,' says Church. 'We were asked to come up with ideas for the composition of the final frame. The design was ball-parked to the point that [the filming crew] had enough to shoot with. For example, they went over to Australia and shot the fight with the monsters in the arena, but at that stage they really had no idea what all that stuff in the background would look like. Sequences like this, and those in the droid foundry, were areas where we were able to contribute our ideas.'

Church and Tiemens largely use programs such as Photoshop and Painter, often painting directly over digital files from the animatics team and digitally captured plates of actors in front of blue-screen backgrounds. 'What's it like to visit this space?' says Tiemens, describing the unusual challenges of their job. 'How do we want to feel? What's the mood and time of day that we want to evoke? Do we want to have a lot of atmosphere in a shot, or do we want striking shadows?'

Computers offer the artists the ability to be highly productive under short deadlines, and the flexibility to quickly adapt the composition or colours of illustrations according to Lucas's wishes. 'We work at gut level,' says Tiemens. 'ILM takes our images and turns them into something that the audience will accept as real.'

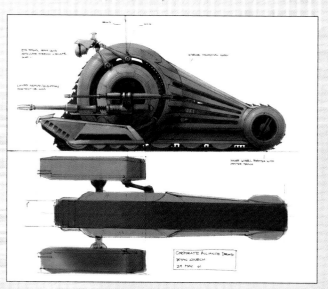

DOUG CHIANG
Concept Design Artist

'My life before *Star Wars* was *Star Wars*, believe it or not,' says Doug Chiang, laughing. 'Throughout my whole career prior to *Star Wars* I was trying to bring my skill levels up to the same level of the *Star Wars* theme.'

Doug is a former creative director at ILM, and was the design director for *The Phantom Menace*. He started work as design director on *Attack of the Clones* a mere week-and-a-half before the release of *The Phantom Menace*.

Chiang worked closely with George Lucas, and later with Gavin Bocquet, in visualising much of the film's hardware and many of its settings. Chiang assembled the art department at Skywalker Ranch and supervised the designers, as well as continuing to design himself.

Chiang had meetings with Lucas every Friday wherein the previous week's work was reviewed (conversations were conducted via conference calls during the filming in Australia and England). 'George always throws down the gauntlet every time he comes in,' said Chiang during production. 'Every Friday he says, "Show me something different." George knows a lot of history, a lot of cultures, and for us to try and come up with a fresh idea when he wants it is a very daunting task.'

The schedule for *Attack of the Clones* was considerably shorter than that of *The Phantom Menace*. 'We have about a third less time, if not even less,' said Chiang. 'Everything is just a little bit quicker, a little more streamlined. We all kind of know how George likes to work, so that just makes things a lot easier. And we can anticipate problems earlier and fix them.'

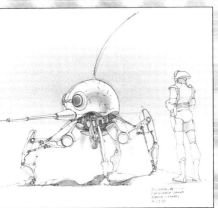

KAMINO CONCEPT ART

Ryan Church and Erik Tiemens studied George Lucas's movie *THX 1138* when visualising the clinical whites and iridescent glows that characterise Tipoca City.

'We're working in a virtual digital feature, and we have to think about backgrounds and other things that haven't been built,' says Tiemens. 'The colour and the look of everything needs to be figured out – we'll know, for example, that there are areas, like on Kamino, where the watery blues and greens can have a nice contrast to larger sequences of the hot reds and oranges that we see later on in the Geonosian landscape. So, just by keeping those things in mind we know how to take a look at the overall colour arcs, the highs and lows, and support where we're at with the storytelling.'

BOBA FETT'S COCKPIT

GENERAL VIEWS (Based on medium size version)

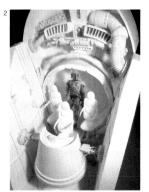

MODELS AND SCULPTURES

Although Lucasfilm and ILM have moved yet further into the digital realm for *Attack of the Clones*, there was still room for the more conventional disciplines of model-making and sculpting in the pre-production process.

The team of concept model-makers included John Duncan and John Goodson. 'John Duncan and John Goodson are probably two of the best conceptual modellers I've ever worked with,' says Doug Chiang. 'They have just an incredible ability to translate two-dimensional drawings into three-dimensional objects that are in many ways far superior to the original designs. They always contribute and add something more. It's an important function, because once we get something approved on paper, we need to visualise it very quickly three dimensionally.'

Duncan and Goodson were responsible for helping to envision the droids, vehicles and starships first described in Lucas's script for Episode II.

'Certain effects supervisors, like John Knoll, love to have models,' says Goodson. 'Even if he's going to do the whole sequence in CG he loves to have models for lighting reference and shadows and all that stuff. I think it's much harder to see things when you design in a computer. I call it going from hands-on to hands-tied because you can put a design on a computer, and put it on a turntable, but it is not the same thing as being able to take it out and hold it in your hand and look at it. Models are little version of reality.'

The production of Episode II saw an increased use of miniature sets. Fellow model-makers Carol Bauman and Kim Smith created table-top sets and cut-out figures that Lucas used to block out scenes before the models were digitally scanned by ILM. 'The set models have turned out to be playsets for George for staging scenes. So he can check lighting and positioning and scale,' said Smith.

Robert Barnes, Tony McVey, and Mike Murnane created numerous sculptures, or maquettes, based on drawings by concept artists. The maquettes were submitted to Lucas for his approval before being painted and then sent to ILM for scanning.

Where the schedule permitted, Barnes preferred to rationalise his designs as much as possible. 'I do spend a lot of time figuring out the pose, and really try to consider what the creature is going to be doing in the scene and what it symbolises to George. I try to nail that in as many ways as possible, from the structure of the anatomy or the actual posture, and try to deliver an animated pose.'

EXT CORUSCANT STREETS / ALLEYWAYS
BUILDING 2
Concept and Model

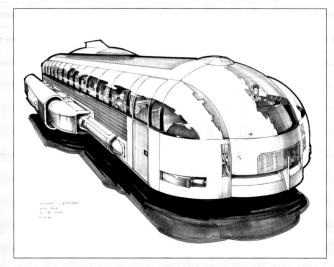

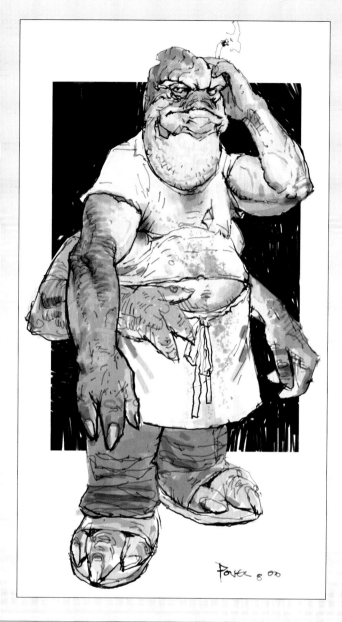

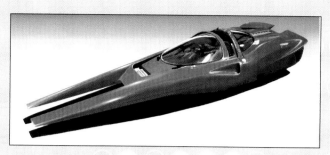

PADME'S APT - MAIN COLOURWAYS

SUGGESTED COLOURWAY FOR MAIN AREA AND BEDROOM

Primarily in the light and dark grey/blues. David Tattersall would prefer the walls and ceilings in the MAIN AREA to be these lighter tones, which will help him in the dusk scene.

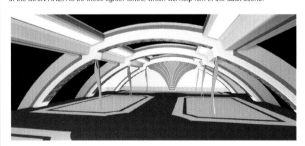

INT HOMESTEAD DINING ROOM

Photo from recent recce

WHITE WASH LINE RAISED

GEONOSIS ROCK COLOUR / TEXTURE

Preliminary Approved Geonasis Locations - Australia / Tunisia?

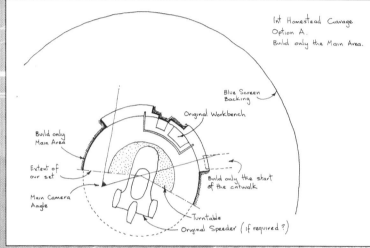

BOBA FETT'S APARTMENT - KAMINO

ALTERNATIVE DOOR DESIGNS

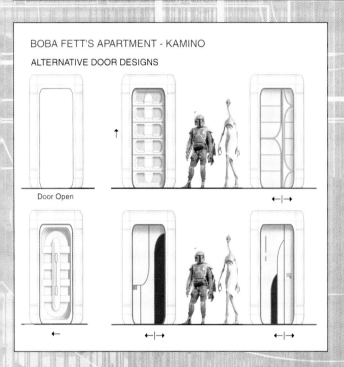

Door Open

Int Homestead Garage
Option A.
Build only the Main Area.

Blue Screen
Backing

Original Workbench

Build only
Main Area

Extent of
our set

Build only the start
of the catwalk

Main Camera
Angle

Turntable

Original Speeder (if required?)

PRODUCTION DESIGN

Gavin Bocquet's team prepared these and many other illustrations to establish the details of objects and sets that needed to be constructed. These objects included furniture and other props that actors needed to physically interact with. Production designs also helped establish how much of each particular set had to be built, and how much could therefore be digitally augmented by Industrial Light & Magic.

SPY DROID SIZE VARIATIONS

THREE ALTERNATIVE 'SPY DROID' SIZE VARIATIONS

BASKETBALL   +10%   +20%

DINER - CORUSCANT

STYLE VARIATIONS

The approved sketched show two distinct styles for the interior. Do you have a preference?

STYLE A - More Industrial / Techy / Grungy

STYLE B - More '50's / Traditional Shapes

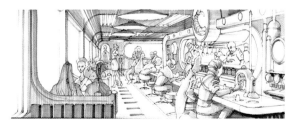

top with outer
layer removed

hair as
Sample sent

armband 1

Larger Utility
holster

armband 2

Boot type 1

Boot type 2
In white -adapted from
Ep 1 Naboo military boot

COSTUME DESIGN

These pages show previously unseen costume designs for Padmé Amidala, Count Dooku and Cliegg Lars.

The costumes for *Attack of the Clones* were sketched by concept artists Iain McCaig and Dermot Power, and created by Trisha Biggar. McCaig had worked with Biggar on *The Phantom Menace*, and on *Attack of the Clones* she was closely involved in the creative process, joining the team at an early stage. 'She saved months of work,' says McCaig. 'I could do a very quick scribble and run it past Trish to see if we were even in the realms of reality. She would say yes or no and suggest alternatives.'

McCaig explains that there is a more adult attitude to Padmé's costumes in *Attack of the Clones*. 'There's a very different sensibility in this one, and it's reflected in Padmé's wardrobe. Obviously, the kids are older now and it's a love story. There's a sexy, seductive element in the film. It's a lot more romantic. And so the costumes we were looking at didn't have to hide Natalie Portman this time. In fact, it was more about how much to reveal! And there's a whole new flavour to the film as a result.'

The art department has created many designs that are yet to be seen. 'We had three years to design Episode I as opposed to one year for Episode II,' says McCaig. 'In those three years, we designed almost all three of the films, and there are thousands of costumes and creatures and ships and things that are approved but just never used. We knew we could draw on that when it came to do the later films.'

The small red 'OK' and 'Fabulouso' stamps are added by George Lucas to artwork he likes.

OK

FABULOUSO

Below: A sequence of animatics showing the shockwaves from a Geonosian blaster in the execution arena.
Right and opposite top: Animatic image and finalframe illustrating Obi-Wan's encounter with Taun We at Tipoca City.
Opposite middle and bottom: Animatics images and final frames from scenes set on Tatooine and Coruscant.

ANIMATICS

Animatics is a process that uses video-resolution computer graphics to previsualise shots or sequences prior to filming or the creation of visual effects. Previsualisation/effects supervisors David Dozoretz and Dan Gregoire liken the result to a moving sketchpad version of the film – more expressive than a traditional storyboard and several notches down from the sophistication of a finished ILM shot.

While hand-illustrated storyboards were still prepared for Episode II – most notably for the end battle sequence – animatics have gone some way towards replacing them as a means to convey the pace and scale of an unfinished sequence.

The animatics team on Episode II included artists Brad Alexander, Eisung Lee, and Matthew Ward. The team produced over 2800 shots for Episode II (over 4000 including the numerous variations and alterations) and found themselves in the thick of the editing process as their material was intercut with live-action footage while the film was being assembled.

'In Episode I the digital animatics were there to get the point of the shot across in a more dynamic way than storyboards could provide,' says Dan Gregoire. 'In Episode II we still wanted to help George answer the question "Will the shot work?", but we also wanted to answer many more of the tough questions before post production began. For example, we indicated the positions of the digital characters such as Jar Jar, Watto, and the Geonosians in blue-screen plates. It can be tough to tell whether material like that will cut back and forth with the live action footage and that's where animatics can help.'

Animatics, which are created on PCs and Macs, can illustrate numerous angles or options for realising a sequence within a much shorter period of time than was previously possible. An example of this flexibility was the animatic version of the airspeeder chase on Coruscant, which initially lasted around 25 minutes.

'The 350 animatic shots we did for the final battle sequences only took the team three weeks,' says Gregoire proudly. 'And that was with full dynamic simulation, particle missile trails, explosions – you name it. For sequences like that we started to define aesthetic qualities as well – the lighting, mood, and the feel. We can show where the sun will be setting and how dense the haze of smoke over the battle will be. These are all elements we can give George control over very early in the process.'

SPY DROID - PADME'S APT

ALTERNATIVE DESIGNS FOR SPY DROID

VERSION C

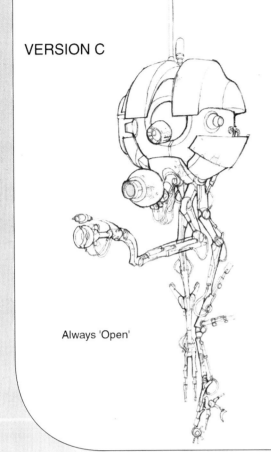

Always 'Open'

VERSION D
SLIGHT DEPARTURE

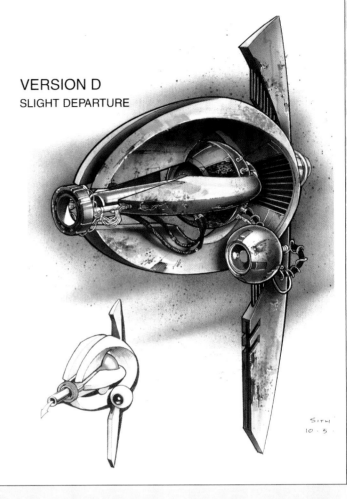

SITH
10 · 5 ·

Top: Production designs of Zam's droid.
Above and right: Evocative illustrations of Coruscant low-life by
Dermot Power.
Opposite: Further concept art, and an overhead view of the Outlander
gambling club set at Fox Studios.

CORUSCANT CONCEPT ART

'Just like the other *Star Wars* movies, it seems that the colour schemes of the skies and the environments all seem to be very deliberately picked by George to reflect and mirror the story,' says Ryan Church. 'It's very subjective, visual storytelling. It's the visuals that support the script and what's going on. There are foreboding colour schemes and foreboding atmospheres that go with the story as well.'

Church recalls that, 'George asked us to break Coruscant down into several neighbourhoods. He told us that he envisioned the city working on a number of levels, from the financial district on the upper levels, moving down to the utility district and finally down to the entertainment district.'

'We gave a colour distinction to each level,' adds Erik Tiemens, 'with the richer, warmer colours on the lower levels. From the beginning of the movie it's clear that Coruscant is a less welcoming, less glamorous place than it seemed in *The Phantom Menace*.'

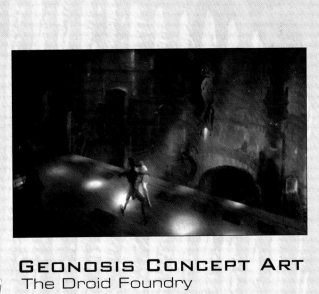

GEONOSIS CONCEPT ART
The Droid Foundry

'We had a short meeting with George and a representative from animatics,' remembers Erik Tiemens. 'George gave us a broad verbal description of the droid foundry and told us we would work our way down from the landscape of Geonosis, beneath the surface of the planet.'

Storyboards were prepared, and formed the precursor to the filming of those sequences at Elstree Studios. Ryan Church and Erik Tiemens then visited an automated car production plant to seek inspiration. 'Car factories can be pretty threatening places,' says Church. 'We knew that it would be great to extrapolate those surroundings into the *Star Wars* universe.'

The Arena

'We were a little more committed to scale with the arena than we had been with the droid foundry,' says Tiemens.

'The scenes had been shot and the landmarks were set,' adds Church. 'We had animatics that showed camera positions and the areas where the reek, the acklay, and the nexu would run. We had sketches from Doug and [fellow concept artist] Ed Natividad, and we had George's descriptions of the termite-like Geonosians.'

Tiemens recalls how Lucas had explained that the Geonosians had carved the arena from solid rock and constructed elaborate towers on the surface of the planet. 'The more we looked into it the more we realised that the aesthetic of Geonosian architecture was very important. Imagine a Gothic church still under construction, sculpted out of the side of a sandstone mountain. We're manipulating recognisable architectural forms, but tempering that with something more naturalistic and organic. On top of all that we were rendering it, creating more polished areas such as the royal box and making other areas look distressed.'

'We had to role-play a bit, trying to think like Geonosians,' says Church, smiling. 'We knew they had the technology to create these incredible robots, but we also knew they were termite-like creatures with wings who lived on a very dry planet. Working with all those assumptions, and bearing in mind the practicalities of filming and visual effects, we had to ask ourselves, "What would Geonosian architecture look like?"'

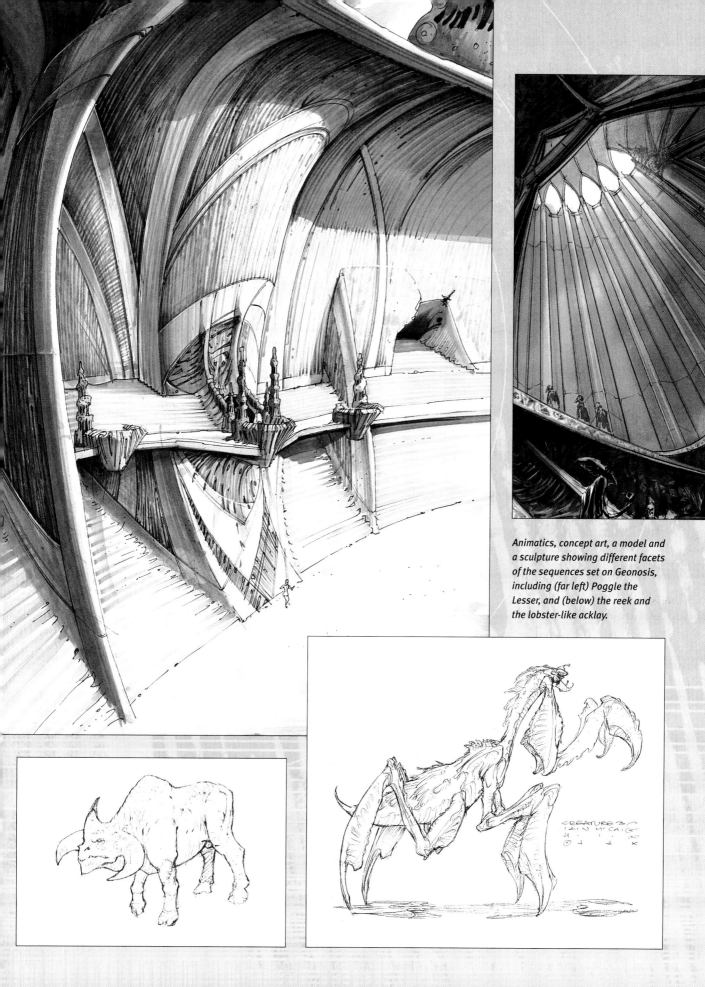

Animatics, concept art, a model and a sculpture showing different facets of the sequences set on Geonosis, including (far left) Poggle the Lesser, and (below) the reek and the lobster-like acklay.

CREATURE 3
IAIN McCAIG
4·1·00

VEHICLE CONCEPT ART

Ryan Church had studied transportation design as a student, and jumped at the opportunity to design some of the vehicles for the end battle sequence. Together with Erik Tiemens he spent time researching World War I vehicles – especially the early tanks used on the Western Front – and gained valuable insight from George Lucas.

'George would ask us, "What came before the [AT-AT] walker in *The Empire Strikes Back*?",' says Church. 'This would set us thinking. I came up with a walker, and Erik designed a stationary artillery gun. George had the idea of putting the gun on top of the walker, and it worked beautifully. If the AT-AT was a mid-eighties sports car then the six-legged walker is a 1958 Buick. It's a lot clunkier. I wanted to create something that the audience would identify as a prototype.'

Church recalls that the missile-launching *Hailfire* started life with rather fewer armaments. 'George would say, "We need something with tank treads, something with wheels." I presented this sketch, which at the time we just called 'The Hula-Hoop Thing', and George asked us to add some missiles on the top. As time went on, he kept asking us to add more and more missiles, and now I can't see it any other way!'

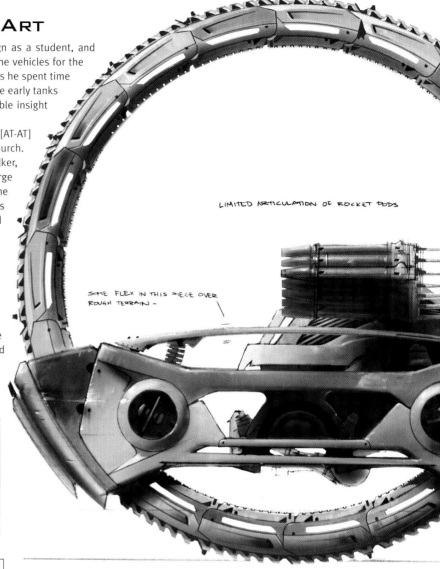

LIMITED ARTICULATION OF ROCKET PODS

SOME FLEX IN THIS PIECE OVER ROUGH TERRAIN –

INNER WHEEL WITH MAIN T

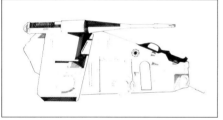

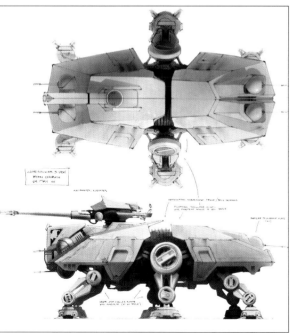

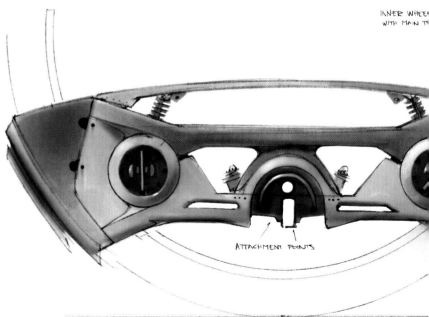

ATTACHMENT POINTS

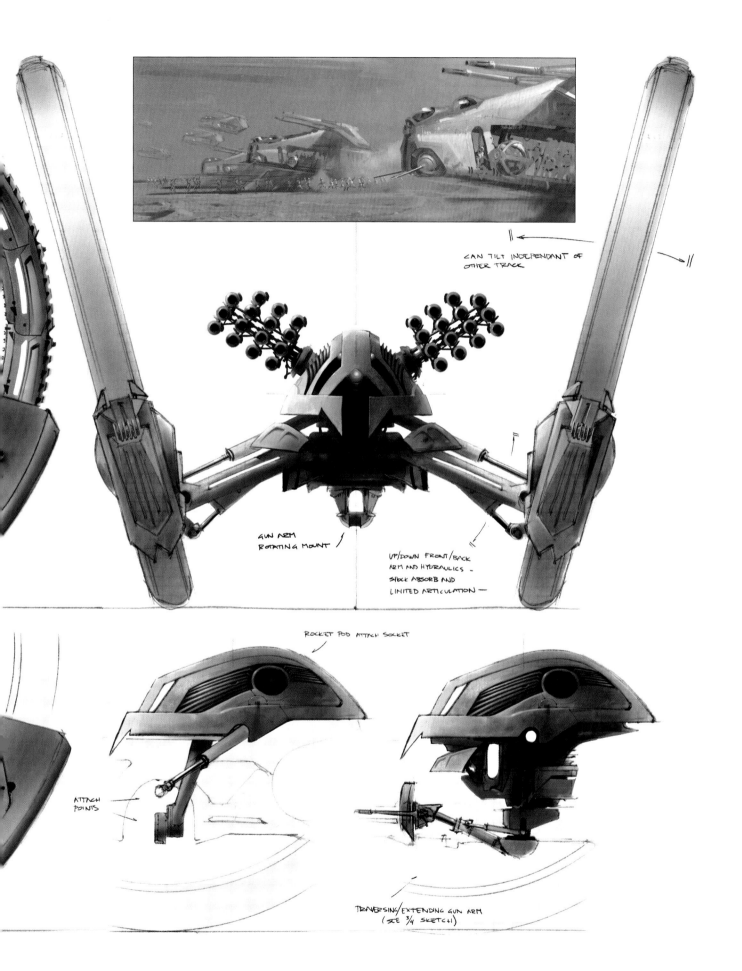

CAN TILT INDEPENDANT OF
OTHER TRACK

GUN ARM
ROTATING MOUNT

UP/DOWN FRONT/BACK
ARM AND HYDRAULICS -
SHOCK ABSORB AND
LIMITED ARTICULATION —

ROCKET POD ATTACH SOCKET

ATTACH
POINTS

TRAVERSING/EXTENDING GUN ARM
(SEE ¾ SKETCH)

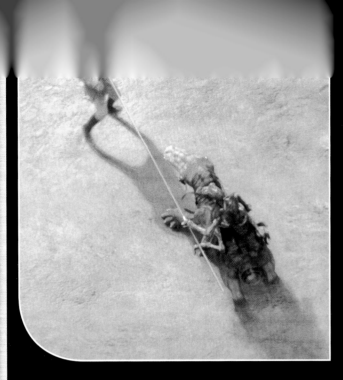

'Let the executions begin!'

PADMÉ, ANAKIN, AND OBI-WAN are accused of espionage and sentenced to execution before a crowd of jeering Geonosians. They are chained to posts in the middle of an arena and watch helplessly as three slavering beasts – the reek, the nexu, and the acklay – are unleashed.

Picadors prod the beasts towards their prey with blue electric bolts as Count Dooku, Poggle the Lesser, and Nute Gunray watch with eager anticipation. The sport that unfolds, however, is not what they expected.

Anakin dodges the charging reek, which collides with the post. Anakin jumps on the reek's back, wrapping his chains around its horn. Obi-Wan ducks around his post, but the force of the acklay's collision sends the Jedi flying. The nexu rears on its hind legs, threatening Padmé. She has already started loosening her chains, and is standing on top of her post.

Obi-Wan grabs a picador's spear and polevaults to safety. Anakin begins to ride the reek, which tries to buck him as the nexu tears the shirt from Padmé's back and scratches her skin. She defends herself by swinging her chains.

Obi-Wan spears the acklay and, just as the nexu is about to leap, Padmé jumps on to the back of the reek behind Anakin. Obi-Wan soon joins them.

There is discord in the royal box, but the Separatist conspirators soon have more to worry about than the fate of their errant prisoners. Mace Windu arrives from Coruscant with almost two hundred peacekeeping Jedi. They take positions all around the arena, and when he gives the signal they ignite their lightsabers *en masse*.

The crowd falls silent....

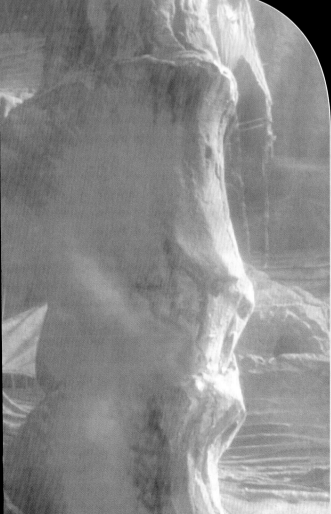

FILMMAKERS

GEORGE LUCAS
Writer, Director, Executive Producer

In February 2000 George Lucas, the creator of *Star Wars*, visited the University of California in Berkeley for an informal question-and-answer session. Many of the questions inevitably centred on the next two chapters in the *Star Wars* prequel trilogy. 'I'm climbing this big mountain,' Lucas said, 'which has taken me ten years at a stretch to do. Right now I'm just concentrating on getting up the mountain. I've got two more films to finish, and then I'll be at the top.'

This innovative filmmaker's journey began at the University of Southern California, where Lucas studied English, Philosophy and took two film classes. Lucas turned heads with the student film *Electronic Labyrinth THX 1138 4EB*, a bizarre collision of futuristic imagery cut to a soundtrack of air traffic control noise and Bach. Lucas won a scholarship to Warner Bros, where he shadowed Francis Ford Coppola during the making of *Finian's Rainbow* (1968). He later collaborated with Coppola on *The Rain People* (1969).

Lucas became friends with Coppola, who was perhaps the first to recognise and champion Lucas's talent. The two formed a production company called American Zoetrope and, in 1970, Lucas directed its first movie – a feature film version of *THX 1138*. The film met with a hostile reaction from distributor Warner Bros, and Coppola had to take a job for hire in order to reimburse them for their investment in the project (it was a little movie called *The Godfather*).

Coppola urged Lucas to write with more warmth and humour for his next project. The result was *American Graffiti* (1973), a semi-autobiographical piece set in 1962. Universal agreed to finance the film as a low-budget picture, and Lucas directed much of it in breathless style. 'He shot everything with two cameras in such a way that you never knew if you were on screen or not, so you gave 100 per cent every time he ran through a scene,' remembers Ron Howard, one of the film's stars. 'He said, "I'm not really getting a chance to direct this film now. I don't have time. I'm really going to direct it in the editing room. That's where I'm going to make all my choices."'

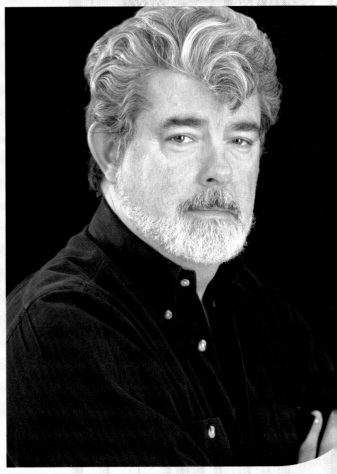

Top: George Lucas directs the cantina sequence from the original *Star Wars* in summer 1976.
Opposite bottom: Lucas with his friend and collaborator Steven Spielberg during the filming of *Indiana Jones and the Temple of Doom*.

Like *THX 1138*, *American Graffiti* met with a hostile reaction from its distributor and was taken out of its director's hands for re-editing. Unlike *THX*, however, *American Graffiti* was a huge commercial success, bringing Lucas acclaim and financial security. The film also brought him to the attention of Hollywood's major players, allowing him to embark on his most ambitious project to date: *Star Wars*.

At one point, Lucas had wanted to make a big screen version of 1930s classic film serial *Flash Gordon*. Unable to obtain the rights, he retained the serial motif but added fast-paced action to the mix. Rejecting feasibility based science fiction of the kind that had informed Kubrick's *2001: A Space Odyssey* (1968), Lucas instead created American cinema's first new mythology since the demise of the Western. Film critics point to other acknowledged references such as Joseph Campbell's book *The Hero's Journey* and Akira Kurosawa's film *The Hidden Fortress* (1958), but the fact remains that *Star Wars* and its two sequels, *The Empire Strikes Back* (1980) and *Return of the Jedi* (1983), were like nothing the world had ever seen before.

Lucas also co-produced and co-created the *Indiana Jones* trilogy of films, which were directed by his friend Steven Spielberg. *Raiders of the Lost Ark* (1981), *Indiana Jones and the Temple of Doom* (1984) and *Indiana Jones and the Last Crusade* (1989) presented an unlikely mix of archaeology and James Bond-style adventure. Lucas is a fiercely independent filmmaker, and his been successful enough to operate outside the studio system for nearly 30 years.

Lucasfilm's independence has allowed its chairman to pursue his ambitions without the added stress of executives looking over his shoulder. Between *Return of the Jedi* in 1983 and the resumption of the *Star Wars* saga in the late 1990s, he produced or executive produced such diverse films as *Howard the Duck* (1986), *Willow* (1988), *Tucker: The Man and His Dream* (1988) and *Radioland Murders* (1994). 'You can only expect about maybe ten per cent of the movies to be successful,' he admits, before adding, 'I've never made a movie *I'm* not happy with.'

Lucas is especially proud of his critically acclaimed television series *The Young Indiana Jones Chronicles*, which premiered in 1992. He has revealed that future projects will also have an historical basis. 'It will be pretty esoteric. I don't know how popular it'll be, but it's something I want to do. I figure that when I get done with *Star Wars*, I'll have earned the right to do it. I will have put together my own stockpile of production money to do pretty much whatever I want to do.'

But for now, Lucas's long-awaited return to directing continues with Episodes II and III of the saga that challenged Hollywood – and won. Rick McCallum confirms that Lucas's directing style remains essentially unchanged, even though he is no longer acting under the same constraints he experienced on *American Graffiti*. '[His style is] loose, fast, intense, and very, very focused,' he says. 'He knows exactly what he needs to do to get into the editing room and he can't wait to get there.'

Lucas has also maintained his love affair with new technology, pushing back the frontiers of computer generated imaging (CGI) and photography during the production of Episode II. 'He's funny, he's insightful, and he has a lot of information about the technical aspect of what's going on,' says *Attack of the Clones* star Samuel L Jackson. 'He was talking about the water in *The Perfect Storm*, and he was so overjoyed that they finally got water right in CGI - it was like watching a kid discover the fact he could actually count or tie his shoes.'

'Five years from now I'm going to be doing a lot of different things,' Lucas told his audience at Berkeley. 'Most of it will probably be television because I like that a lot. And more Internet television which I'm trying to put together.'

Lucas may be looking forward to finally scaling his *Star Wars* mountain, but there are clearly further challenges on the horizon.

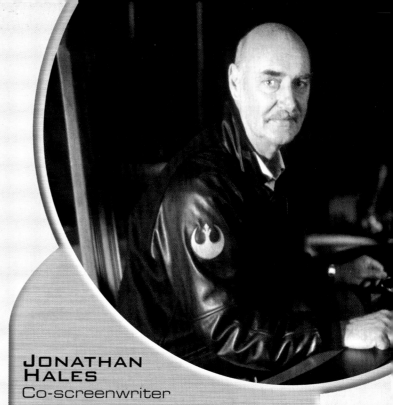

JONATHAN HALES
Co-screenwriter

British writer Jonathan Hales had previously scripted George Lucas's story for the opening episode of *The Young Indiana Jones Chronicles*. Hales ultimately wrote or co-wrote seven episodes of the award-winning series. 'I just loved it,' he says. 'It's such a brilliant idea that Henry Jones Jr was born on 1 July 1899, so in fact his life story is actually the history of the 20th century. The main challenge was to actually try and come anywhere near the scope of the idea.'

Hales was reunited with Lucas in April 2000, when he helped refine the screenplay for Episode II into its final drafts. 'My personal goal was to make it the best screenplay that ever was, so that it will be the best movie that ever was,' he says.

'I tried to forget, in a way, that it was *Star Wars*, in a sense that I didn't want to think, "Oh my God, there is a world out there waiting to see this stuff." I just tried to concentrate on it and what it was, and forget about that terrifying dimension that's out there.'

RICK McCALLUM
Producer

Rick McCallum has enjoyed collaborations with such notable filmmakers as playwright Dennis Potter and director Nicolas Roeg. Since 1990, McCallum has worked exclusively with George Lucas, overseeing the complex and demanding production of *The Young Indiana Jones Chronicles* (four years shooting in 27 countries) and *Radioland Murders*, a long-cherished Lucas project that was directed by Mel Smith and released in 1994.

McCallum produced the Special Editions of the *Star Wars* trilogy in 1997. Like his previous two Lucasfilm projects, these remastered, remixed and reinvigorated versions of the original classics proved the potential of digital special effects. Just as importantly, however, the Special Editions also proved the *Star Wars* saga's enduring box office appeal and paved the way for Episodes I to III.

McCallum worked hard to keep to the demanding schedule of Episode II, giving his director the space he needed. 'The work is always very intense,' he says. 'You deal with the daily issues that are painful and complex. We really do everything in our power not to have the kind of tense, uptight, crazy atmosphere where there are egos running around. That isn't the world and the environment that we've got here.'

Having produced the Special Editions as well as the prequel trilogy, McCallum is looking forward to having made a crucial contribution to every film in the series. 'Ultimately in 2006 or 2007 or sometime, you are going to be able to go into a theatre at midday and come out 12 hours later and see it all. That's my dream. I don't know that it's anybody's plan. Digitally projected, Episode I through VI in a row. That's what makes it *The Godfather* in another galaxy.'

BEN BURTT
Editor

Ben Burtt's sound design made an enormous contribution to the original *Star Wars* trilogy. Burtt created the beeps and whistles of R2-D2, the roar of the Empire's TIE fighters, and the humming crackles of clashing lightsabers.

Burtt spent 15 years as a sound designer for Lucasfilm, and went freelance in 1990. *The Young Indiana Jones Chronicles* became a vehicle for his many talents – he acted as a film and sound editor on certain episodes, directed first and second units on others, and even co-wrote the feature length instalment, *Attack of the Hawkmen*.

Burtt co-edited *The Phantom Menace*, in addition to his sound design duties, and spent over 18 months at the helm of an Avid workstation working towards the final cut of *Attack of the Clones*. Surrounded by classic movie posters in a darkened room at Skywalker Ranch, director and editor painstakingly compiled *Attack of the Clones* from a bewildering tapestry of live action and special effects sequences. The unprecedented flexibility and accessibility of digital photography enabled Burtt to begin work in summer 2000, while principal photography was still underway. He started editing using the art department's animatics sequences, and had already assembled 60 or 70 per cent of what had been shot in Sydney before Lucas ultimately joined him in California. The assembly cut, distilled from over 100 hours of digital 'footage', formed the basis of the director's first rough cut.

'George is directing in the editing room,' said Burtt. 'He may rewrite something or re-conceive a scene. It's also the first time that he's had a chance to review his footage and reflect on it. Now, he can sit back

and forget that stress of directing on-set, and instead evaluate and critique what he's got. Not only do you have every shot to pass judgement on, but also every pixel within every shot. There's nothing to stop you from moving things around, changing lighting, or altering sets, splitting characters up and rearranging things. That's what's happening now. It's his usual process, which is to take apart what he's done, and experiment with what he's got.'

GAVIN BOCQUET
Production Designer

'Basically what I do as production designer in breaking down the script is understanding an environment and what happens in it,' says Gavin Bocquet. 'Who comes in? What characters are there coming in this door or that door, or flying through the door. You need all that information since it's all part of the design process. You must know all the visual and functional cues for shooting.'

Bocquet began his career as an art department draughtsman on *The Elephant Man* and *Return of the Jedi*. Since then, his more senior credits have included *Empire of the Sun* (1987), *Dangerous Liaisons* (1988), and *Kafka* (1991). He received an Emmy for his work on *The Young Indiana Jones Chronicles* and also worked on *Radioland Murders* and *The Phantom Menace* for Lucasfilm. *Attack of the Clones* offered the fresh challenges of two previously unseen worlds (Kamino and Geonosis) which, as before, had to be constructed in a way that seamlessly dovetailed with ILM's digital augmentation.

'I think that probably amongst the people who have done it before, there is a sort of comfort blanket that came with doing the first one,' he said during filming. 'Doing the first *Star Wars*, after doing *Young Indy*, was a whole new experience for all of us. It was first thing ever of that size for us. I think we were probably unaware of the slight trepidation we all had while we were doing it. But obviously doing it a second time, you're much more relaxed, even with doing it in another country.'

Bocquet is especially pleased that the script for *Attack of the Clones* featured such relatively intimate locations as Padmé's apartment and the lodge at the Naboo lake retreat. 'They're quite important for us, because you don't often get many personal environments in the *Star Wars* world. There's a nice bit of characterisation you can get in there, which you can't do so much when you're in the rather sterile environments of spacecraft and things like that.'

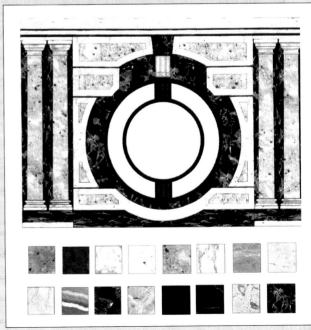

TRISHA BIGGAR
Costume Designer

Although Trisha Biggar has designed costumes for numerous stage and film productions, some of her most prominent pre-*Star Wars* work was in television. She received a BAFTA nomination for her contribution to Granada's earthy adaptation of *Moll Flanders* and designed costumes for *The Young Indiana Jones Chronicles*.

Biggar's work on Episodes I and II has been similarly informed by historical references, although she describes the look of *Attack of the Clones* as being less militaristic than its predecessor. 'We don't have groups or soldiers,' she says. 'In Episode I, we had big groups of Naboo soldiers and Royal Palace Guards. This episode, the costumes are very much more individual. We're going from different planets, so we have Coruscant street people, and it's interesting because they come from all over. On Naboo, we're seeing mostly people who were in and around the palace, and who are a very well dressed middle class; just regular people who live and work on Naboo.'

Biggar reveals that Padmé has even more costumes in *Attack of the Clones* than she wore when she was Queen in *The Phantom Menace*. 'Hard to believe, but yes,' she laughs. 'She has softer clothes, which are less formal. Natalie's also a little bit older, so she has some sexier clothes. It's nice. I think she likes them.'

IAIN McCAIG
DERMOT POWER
Concept Artists

Two of the most prominent new costume designs in the movie belong to Anakin Skywalker and Padmé Amidala. Biggar devised Anakin's new look in collaboration with concept designers Iain McCaig and Dermot Power. 'We really took the shape of Darth Vader's cloak and tried to steer that back to a Jedi style to create a simpler outline than the traditional Jedi cloak,' she recalls. 'We ended up with something that could still definitely be Jedi with the hood, but just with that vaguely familiar outline.'

Iain McCaig began his Lucasfilm career as a concept designer and storyboard artist at ILM and is now a director in his own right. His contribution to Episode I included visualising the look for Darth Maul and many of Queen Amidala's baroque gowns.

Irish-born Dermot Power is a former *2000AD* cover artist who came to the attention of Doug Chiang following the production of Episode I. Power worked closely with McCaig developing the Episode II costumes and eventually shouldered most of the work as McCaig's schedule wound down. He commuted from London to Skywalker Ranch during pre-production, and then joined Trisha Biggar in Sydney. 'She's wonderful to work with,' said Power during production. 'Before I knew it, we'd hit 300 costumes. We'll likely end up with about 1200 in total, about the same number used for Episode I.'

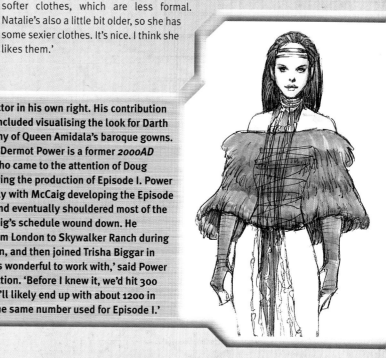

DAVID TATTERSALL
Director of Photography

Director of photography David Tattersall is a veteran of a number of Lucasfilm productions overseen by producer Rick McCallum. Tattersall worked on *The Young Indiana Jones Chronicles* (for which he won an Emmy and ASC nominations for Best Cinematography) and *Radioland Murders* before joining the crew of *The Phantom Menace*.

The director of photography traditionally oversees the camera and lighting crews on a film, but that was the only traditional thing about Tattersall's duties on *Attack of the Clones*. While Tattersall was using film cameras on *The Phantom Menace*, on the new movie he used cameras that recorded a high definition digital image. Unlike film cameras – which need frequent reloading – the digital cameras could run smoothly all day.

One of Tattersall's few concessions to the digital process was a slight softening of the lighting style used in the previous film. This was because tests had showed that the digital cameras were less forgiving in recording certain hard contrasts. The chores of lighting the numerous blue-screen scenes remained the same. 'It's much more fun to light a full environment,' says Tattersall. 'There's no artistry in lighting blue-screen; it's just a technical process.'

Tattersall referred to concept illustrations to get an indication of how the digital sets and backdrops would ultimately look. 'Those helped me because they gave me some ideas as to where the light would be coming from.'

George Lucas and Rick McCallum are not the only industry luminaries who admire Tattersall's work – award-winning writer/director Frank Darabont hired him for *The Green Mile* (1999) and *The Majestic* (2001).

NICK GILLARD
Stunt Co-ordinator

Nick Gillard ran away from military school to join the circus when he was just 12. By the time he was 16 he was a world-class horsetrick-rider with the Moscow State Circus, and about to embark on a new career as a stunt man in the film industry.

Three years later, Gillard joined the stunt team on the original *Star Wars*. Gillard returned to the galaxy far, far away 20 years and 35 films later when he became the stunt co-ordinator on Episode I. Since *The Phantom Menace*, Gillard has worked alongside Episode II luminaries Ian McDiarmid and Christopher Lee on *Sleepy Hollow* (1999) and trained Samuel L Jackson for the remake of *Shaft* (2000).

Gillard visited a number of martial arts clubs in and around Sydney to recruit stunt fighters for the *Attack of the Clones*. 'I heard of one group that had been banned from the national competitions because they are way too aggressive,' said Gillard. 'When I heard that, I knew they could be right for us.'

Gillard devised unique styles of fighting for each actor on *The Phantom Menace*, and he continued to develop that philosophy on *Attack of the Clones* with new moves and new styles for Hayden Christensen, Christopher Lee, and Samuel L Jackson. 'Mace Windu's fighting abilities are second only to Yoda's,' says Gillard, smiling. 'If he gets within range, there's no question... you're dead.'

Gillard is aware that the adult Anakin Skywalker will have to live up to the reputation of his future alter ego Darth Vader. 'Of course, he's the chosen one,' he says. 'The audience will want to see that manifest itself. There needs to be flashes of brilliance. He's more skilled than Obi-Wan. Anakin always attacks. He's better and he knows it, which means he's brash on occasion.'

Above: Nick Gillard coaches some of the young extras for the sequence showing the Bear Clan being trained by Yoda.

JOHN KNOLL
Visual Effects Supervisor

John Knoll enjoys a reputation as one of the foremost exponents of digital effects technology. Outside the film industry, Knoll is best known as one of the original authors of the image-manipulation software Photoshop, which is the leading computer graphics package for professional and home users alike. Knoll describes his programming achievements as, 'one in a series of hobbies I turned into a profession.'

Knoll's distinguished career at Industrial Light & Magic began when he was a motion-control camera operator on the 1986 film *Captain Eo*. Knoll went on to become the computer graphics project designer on James Cameron's groundbreaking movie *The Abyss* (1989). ILM was honoured with its tenth Academy Award for the film's outstanding visual effects.

Knoll was a visual effects supervisor on the *Star Wars Trilogy Special Edition* and *The Phantom Menace*, and was one of four ILM experts to lead the visual effects teams in *Attack of the Clones*. His team was responsible for creating elements of the airspeeder chase in Coruscant, the asteroid field dogfight around Geonosis, and the arena sequence on Geonosis.

The planets and types of shots required presented a variety of challenges to ILM's expertise and schedule. 'Shots vary quite a bit,' said Knoll. 'Some just take a few hours. If it's just, "Here, put a lightsaber in here, and paint something out of the corner," those are really easy and you can do many of them in a day. On the other hand, our first airspeeder chase shot – a big wide view of the city – took a couple of months.'

PABLO HELMAN
Visual Effects Supervisor

Argentinean-born Pablo Helman was ILM's Sabre supervisor on *Deep Impact* (1998), *Saving Private Ryan* (1998), and *October Sky* (1999). Helman is quick to point out that Sabre is a digital compositing and editing tool and has nothing to do with the Jedi weapon, although his duties on Episode I did include adding the light-saber effects for the climactic duel between Qui-Gon, Obi-Wan, and Darth Maul.

Helman is now a fully fledged visual effects supervisor at ILM, and worked on the Jack Nicholson movie *The Pledge* (2001). His team on *Attack of the Clones* included 120 visual effects artists. They were responsible for some of the key scenes on Tatooine, various shots of Yoda, and the fight between Obi-Wan and Jango Fett.

'On a film like this, everything is effects work because every shot involves effects,' said Helman. 'The film is being shot in high definition, so every shot is being touched digitally somehow.

'I don't think the public, the audience, will be able to tell whether it was shot on film or not, because it looks like film. When you look at it on a digital projection system the colours are incredible, very saturated and film-like.'

Despite his considerable technical knowledge, Helman claims to spend 80 per cent of his working day talking to people. 'There's a lot of problem-solving,' he said. 'I don't have time to be surprised because of the kind of schedule we have and the volume of work. I have to take it day by day. I don't think about the whole project – if I do, I panic!'

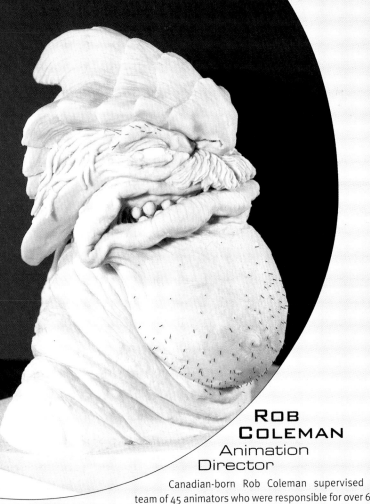

ROB COLEMAN
Animation Director

Canadian-born Rob Coleman supervised a team of 45 animators who were responsible for over 60 digital creatures in *The Phantom Menace*, including Jar Jar Binks, Watto and Podrace cheat Sebulba.

Coleman's team began preliminary work on *Attack of the Clones* in early summer 2000, and benefited from their leader's unparalleled experience. 'My metaphor for making the movie is pretty much the same as the last one, which is an enormously huge train which takes a long time to get going and then reaches terminal velocity and heads towards a 14-foot concrete wall at maximum speed. So when we're rolling about a year from now the train's going about 95 miles an hour and it's racing through the stations and nothing can stop it.'

Coleman oversaw the realisation of 80 digital characters for *Attack of the Clones*. These included familiar creatures such as Jar Jar and Watto, and new creations such as Dexter Jettster and the beasts in the Geonosis arena.

'We have about 150 more shots in animation than we did last time,' said Coleman. 'My group makes the character walk or deliver its line, or shoot a gun, or jump out a window – whatever it needs to do. A lot of the most difficult acting shots are when there is no dialogue, and it's a character just looking or reacting to what's said in the room. They need to have emotions and thoughts. We spend time on those shots.'

FRED MEYERS
HD Supervisor

Fred Meyers joined ILM in 1990 to build the video engineering department and design the company's electronic rushes and digital editorial systems. He went on to combine the computer, video, and production software support groups into one overall area. Meyers currently leads the special projects for ILM's parent company Lucas Digital and has been at the forefront of research into the integration of high definition video into feature film production.

Meyers took delivery of a prototype of the high definition camera at ILM a year before the shooting of Episode II was scheduled to begin. 'The benefits were clear even before we started the final, intensive test,' says Meyers. 'The system offered David Tattersall and his team the same tools they had before, with the added advantage of immediate feedback. We set up engineering stations on set and on location, and we saw the dailies with synchronised sound while we were shooting. It meant editing could begin almost immediately.'

Meyers is used to being asked whether digital photography is the way forward for all filmmakers. 'That's the $64,000 question,' he says, laughing. 'I think it's inevitable.'

ILM VISUAL EFFECTS PRODUCERS
Judith Weaver

Judith Weaver was the executive visual effects producer for *Attack of the Clones*, overseeing the work of all three ILM units. She had been the senior visual effects producer on *The Perfect Storm* (2000), the film that created breakthrough computer-generated water sequences. 'We started work on the Kamino sequences in August 2001, and they took about seven months to complete,' she recalls. 'They would have taken a lot longer if we hadn't had the experience of creating the water for *The Perfect Storm*.'

Weaver confirms that the scale of Episode II is highly unusual. 'On average, one of our usual shows has about 350 shots,' she says. 'This one has about 2,200.'

Jill Brooks

Visual effects producer Jill Brooks was responsible for producing the visual effects for John Knoll's unit, which included shots from the opening Coruscant sequence, the airspeeder chase, and the execution arena battle. Prior to *Attack of the Clones*, Brooks worked on *Memoirs of an Invisible Man* (1992), *Schindler's List* (1993), *The Mask* (1994), *Jumanji* (1995), *Mars Attacks!* (1996), *Deep Impact* (1998), and *Bringing Out the Dead* (1999).

Gretchen Libby

Gretchen Libby produced the visual effects for the unit helmed by Pablo Helman. This team was responsible primarily for creating the worlds of Kamino, Naboo, and Tatooine. Prior to *Attack of the Clones*, Libby produced the visual effects for *The Perfect Storm* and the additional scenes for *The Phantom Menace* DVD.

Heather Macdonald

Heather Macdonald was the visual effects producer for the Ben Snow and Dennis Muren unit, which created the droid foundry and the clone war visual effects. Macdonald's previous production credits include *Forrest Gump* (1994), *Congo* (1995), *Twister* (1996), *Saving Private Ryan* (1998), *The Phantom Menace* and *The Mummy Returns* (2001).

Above: Visual effects executive producer Judith Weaver (second from left), flanked by visual effects producers Jill Brooks (far left), Gretchen Libby (third from left) and Heather Macdonald (far right).

BEN SNOW
Visual Effects Supervisor

Australian visual effects expert Ben Snow is glad he listened to some good advice when he was at school. 'I wanted to get into films,' he remembers, 'but my parents said, "You should study computing because you'll be able to get into anything if you do that." I didn't really believe that was the case, but I was able to get a computing and film degree. A few years later, computer graphics took off, and that's how I got into the film business.'

Snow created some outstanding effects for *The Mummy* (1999) and *Pearl Harbor* (2001) and worked alongside Dennis Muren in creating some of the most demanding digital sequences from the closing sections of *Attack of the Clones*.

The team headed by Ben Snow and visual effects supervisor Dennis Muren concentrated on some spectacular sequences set on Geonosis: the chase through the subterranean droid foundry and the battle between the clones and the Battle Droids on the surface of the planet.

Snow is especially enthused about the confrontation between the clone troopers and the droids outside the execution arena on Geonosis. 'We're doing a really spectacular battle scene,' he said during post-production. 'But of course there are all sorts of different alien machines and tanks and droids, which makes it more challenging. We're working on new technology to help us create the landscapes and all the atmospherics and haze – there's a lot of dust that gets kicked up by that battle!'

Below: Visual effects supervisor Ben Snow (far right) examines a Geonosian spire crafted in the ILM model shop with art director Alex Jaeger (left) and sequence supervisor Hayden Landis (middle).

JOHN WILLIAMS
Composer

Over the course of one of the most accomplished and celebrated careers in the history of motion picture music, John Williams has been nominated for 41 Oscars and won five. Some of the most memorable movie music of the last three decades belongs to him. The ominous cello predicting the onslaught of *Jaws* (1975), the alien signature announcing mankind's *Close Encounters of the Third Kind* (1977) and the heartrending violin that accompanied *Schindler's List* (1993) are just three of Williams's most famous collaborations with Steven Spielberg.

Among Williams's best-known music is the resounding theme from *Star Wars*, which has opened every instalment of the saga. In 2001 he composed a suitably spellbinding score for *Harry Potter and the Philosopher's Stone*, and followed this up with Spielberg's *Minority Report* and *Attack of the Clones*.

Williams began working on *Attack of the Clones* when he visited Skywalker Ranch in the first week of October 2001. He watched a rough cut of the film and discussed its requirements scene-by-scene with George Lucas and editor Ben Burtt. As is customary with *Star Wars*, the London Symphony Orchestra performed the score, which Williams conducted during recording sessions at London's Abbey Road Studios in January 2002.

Williams is already looking forward to Episode III. 'George Lucas has narrated the last piece to me,' he says. 'After I heard it, I told him, "Just hurry up and do it, because this is a fabulous ending." I'm enjoying very good health, and if that continues, I will complete the sixth film. I'm 69 years old. I'd very much like to complete this sixth piece so that this body of *Star Wars* material is rounded off and completed.'

DENNIS MUREN
Visual Effects Supervisor

Dennis Muren is ILM's senior visual effects supervisor, with responsibility for such epoch-making productions as *ET – The Extra Terrestrial* (1982), *Terminator 2: Judgment Day* (1991), and *Jurassic Park* (1993). He was a visual effects camera operator on *Star Wars* (1977), and has supervised visual effects on over 20 films.

The 55-year-old Muren has received eight Academy Awards and was the first visual effects artist to be honoured with a star on Hollywood's Walk of Fame. Despite all this, he has retained his childhood fascination for filmmaking. 'I was very happy being a kid with my camera,' he says, 'lying down on the grass with a plastic dinosaur and taking pictures of it. I guess things haven't changed much since then.'

'You're impossibly outnumbered.'

EVENTS IN THE ARENA on Geonosis balance on a knife-edge as Mace Windu threatens Count Dooku and his Separatist allies. Dooku doesn't take Mace Windu or his peacekeeping Jedi seriously, and gives the command for a thousand Battle Droids to launch an offensive.

Anakin, Obi-Wan, and Padmé join the beleaguered Jedi as they fight bravely against the Battle Droids and the Geonosians. Mace Windu kills Jango Fett, but before long the sheer numbers of blasting droids prove overwhelming and only around 20 Jedi survive the first phase of the battle.

Mace, Obi-Wan, Anakin, and Padmé battle on back-to-back with the other survivors as they are surrounded by droidekas. All around the arena, Battle Droids train their blasters on the hostages, seemingly oblivious to the carnage.

Count Dooku is about to order the execution of the prisoners when six Republic gunships descend from the sky and land in the arena. Clone troopers disembark and open fire on the Battle Droids. Meanwhile, further Republic ships arrive under the command of Yoda. They carry tens of thousands of clone troopers, who engage the Battle Droids with ruthless efficiency.

Poggle the Lesser panics, and orders his troopers to withdraw to the catacombs. The Trade Federation's Rune Haako orders his ships back into space. Dooku decides to return to his Master on Coruscant, taking with him the secret holographic plans for a new Geonosian weapon.

Events outside the arena have long since spiralled out of control. The fierce aerial combat and the deafening sound of the clone troopers' artillery can mean only one thing – the Clone Wars have begun.

OTHER ANAKINS

Jake Lloyd was eight years old when he played Tatooine slave boy Anakin Skywalker in *The Phantom Menace*. Too young to be considered for the role in Episodes II and III, Lloyd has nevertheless kept busy with lead roles in *Madison* (2000) and *Die With Me* (2001).

Numerous actors and stunt performers brought Darth Vader to life in the original *Star Wars* trilogy. The most notable were David Prowse, who embodied Vader's giant presence; Bob Anderson, who performed the lightsaber fights and stunts in *The Empire Strikes Back* and *Return of the Jedi*; James Earl Jones, who provided the character's booming voice; and Sebastian Shaw, who played the unmasked character at the point of his death and ultimate redemption.

THE CAST
HAYDEN CHRISTENSEN
Anakin Skywalker

Hayden Christensen was born in Vancouver in 1981 but raised in Toronto. He started his career acting in commercials aged just seven, and when he was 12, he won a regular role in Canadian soap opera *Family Passions*.

Prior to being cast as Anakin Skywalker, Christensen's most prominent role had been in the Fox Family Channel's *Higher Ground*, a drama series set in a boarding school for rehabilitating teenagers. His film work had included small roles in such films as John Carpenter's *In the Mouth of Madness* (1995) and *The Virgin Suicides* (1999). By coincidence, the latter was directed by Sofia Coppola, a family friend of George Lucas's who had appeared as a handmaiden in *The Phantom Menace*.

Casting director Robin Gurland embarked on a huge search to find the right actor for Anakin, all the time dismissing rumours that well known stars such as Leonardo Di Caprio were even being considered.

Rick McCallum believes that Christensen has a striking presence and charisma: 'I wouldn't say there is anything damaged about Hayden, but there is something about him that makes you think, "Yeah, this guy could lose it."'

Christensen immersed himself in the four previous *Star Wars* films, carefully studying how his predecessors had interpreted the role of Anakin Skywalker/Darth Vader. 'Other people had played him,' he says, 'and as much as I might have liked to make the character my own, I really couldn't.'

During the long post-production period for *Attack of the Clones*, Christensen played a lead role opposite Kevin Kline and Kristin Scott Thomas in Irwin Winkler's comedy drama *Life As a House* (2001). A career in Hollywood beckons, but it is likely that Christensen's thoughts are already focused on the challenges of depicting Anakin's downfall in Episode III.

NATALIE PORTMAN
Padmé Amidala

Natalie Portman was born in Jerusalem in 1981, and emerged as a film star just 13 years later when she gave an astonishing performance as Mathilda, the streetwise companion to Jean Reno's *Leon* (1994). Since then, Portman has appeared in Woody Allen's *Everyone Says I Love You* (1996) and Tim Burton's *Mars Attacks!* (1996). Since playing Queen Amidala in *The Phantom Menace* Portman has largely been concentrating on her college work.

'She is a woman now,' says Rick McCallum. 'She gets to wear sexy costumes and she is much more attuned to who she is and what she wants to be as a person. Her life is balanced. She has a great academic career, so she doesn't take stardom or any of that seriously at any level.'

In *Attack of the Clones* Padmé is free of her cumbersome regal gowns and the heavy burden of office. 'I was very excited she wasn't going to be Queen any more,' says Portman, 'because it allowed the character to be more like a real person, as opposed to this regal façade of a person.'

Portman's performance conveys Padmé's anger, condescension, and finally love during the tumultuous time she spends with her young Jedi bodyguard. 'It starts out that her relationship with Anakin is one of mentor,' says Portman. 'She's known him only as a little boy prior to this episode; so when they re-encounter each other, she treats him like a little kid. George worked with me to make me seem older than Anakin, to make it believable that she would boss him around and look at him as a little boy – at least for the first half of the film, until it becomes more of a romance.'

'I was nervous at first about having a relative newcomer playing the lead in this film. I was scared that he would be intimidated because it was *Star Wars* and he would be working opposite people like Ewan McGregor and Ian McDiarmid. I'd done ten films at that point, and I was still nervous. But Hayden wasn't. He walked on the set very confident in his abilities. He's an incredible actor.'

HARRISON FORD

Harrison Ford made his film debut with a small role in *Dead Heat on a Merry-Go-Round* (1966) and was still a struggling actor when George Lucas cast him as Bob Falfa in *American Graffiti* (1973). *Star Wars*, *Raiders of the Lost Ark* (1981), and *Blade Runner* (1982) assured Ford's status as one of the world's biggest box-office draws. He was nominated for an Academy Award for his performance in *Witness* (1985) and nominated for a Golden Globe for *The Fugitive* (1993).

One of Ford's most recent movies, *What Lies Beneath* (2000), grossed over $100 million in the US alone, and his career shows no sign of flagging. He is still best remembered, however, for his portrayals of Han Solo, the roguish paramour of Princess Leia, and Indiana Jones. Ford professed to being intrigued by the *Star Wars Trilogy Special Edition* (although he expressed light-hearted reservations about seeing '20-year-old acting') and the prospect of a fourth Indiana Jones film remains a tantalising proposition.

CARRIE FISHER

Carrie Fisher was 19 years old (the same age as Natalie Portman during the filming of Episode II) when she was cast as Princess Leia Organa in the first *Star Wars* film. It has subsequently been revealed that Leia is Anakin and Padmé's daughter.

Fisher played a prominent role in all three episodes of the original *Star Wars* trilogy, and now combines acting with a career as a writer. Her novels *Postcards From the Edge*, *Surrender the Pink*, and *Delusions of Grandma* have all become bestsellers, and her screenplays include an adaptation of *Postcards* and an episode of *The Young Indiana Jones Chronicles*.

EWAN McGREGOR
Obi-Wan Kenobi

In *The Phantom Menace*, the uneasy relationship between Obi-Wan and Qui-Gon was underpinned by a strong mutual admiration. In *Attack of the Clones*, Obi-Wan privately acknowledges Anakin's remarkable abilities, but the headstrong Padawan doesn't always show Obi-Wan much respect in return.

Ewan McGregor has lost the Padawan braid he wore in the last film and now has long, shoulder-length hair and a full beard. Other than that, he insists that *Attack of the Clones* is business as usual. 'Obi-Wan is a good guy... he's straight down the line, and that's as much as there is to go on, really. I didn't know what he had been up to in the last ten years, and I didn't think it would help me to find out because the dialogue in this film was immediate. It was all about what was happening right here and now. There wasn't much room for back stories.'

McGregor was born in Crieff, Scotland, in 1971. As any *Star Wars* fan will tell you, he is the nephew of actor Denis Lawson, who played X-wing pilot Wedge Antilles in all three instalments of the original trilogy.

McGregor came to prominence playing a rebellious Foreign Office clerk in Dennis Potter's musical drama *Lipstick On Your Collar*, and made a huge impact in *Shallow Grave* (1994) and *Trainspotting* (1996), two films from the team of Danny Boyle, Andrew MacDonald, and John Hodge. Since then he has largely resisted the conventional path to Hollywood by remaining a star in such prominent British films as *The Velvet Goldmine* and *Little Voice* (both 1998). He was James Joyce in *Nora* (2000), which he also produced, and played opposite Nicole Kidman in Baz Luhrmann's radical reworking of *Moulin Rouge* (2001).

McGregor has fond memories of the day when his four-year-old daughter Clara visited the set and fell in love with R2-D2, claiming she wanted to marry him. 'I don't personally want to marry Artoo,' he says, 'but there is something about him that makes you feel great affection for him. I think it is a combination of his shape and his high-pitched voice. He's just incredibly appealing. In fact, I believe he is George's favourite actor, which is very telling of George!'

LIAM NEESON
Qui-Gon Jinn

Irish actor Liam Neeson brought a commanding presence to his portrayal of Qui-Gon Jinn, Obi-Wan's Master, in *The Phantom Menace*.

Neeson trained to be a teacher, but joined the Lyric Players Theatre in Belfast in 1976. He made his film debut in John Boorman's *Excalibur* four years later, and has since starred in over 20 other films.

Neeson won the role of Qui-Gon even though the character was described as a man in his sixties in the script of *The Phantom Menace*. 'He is almost like a monk,' said Neeson during production, 'an old-time warrior who is wise and quite philosophical, yet very skilled in martial arts. He has incredible confidence, as well as a magical quality that enables him to see into the future.'

Neeson himself declines to look into the future when asked whether the spirit of the slain Qui-Gon will appear in any subsequent *Star Wars* films. He has, however, made the cryptic observation that 'Jedi never die'....

ALEC GUINNESS
Elder Obi-Wan Kenobi

In the original *Star Wars* trilogy the elder Obi-Wan Kenobi was played by one of Britain's most distinguished theatrical knights. Sir Alec Guinness was best remembered for his starring roles in such classic Ealing comedies as *Kind Hearts and Coronets* (1949), *The Man in the White Suit* (1951), and *The Lavender Hill Mob* (1951). His dramatic roles brought him to an international audience, and his most notable performances for David Lean – including *Oliver Twist* (1948) and *Doctor Zhivago* (1965) – are considered some of the highlights of his career. His performance in Lean's *The Bridge on the River Kwai* (1957) earned him an Academy Award.

Guinness's faith in George Lucas and the screenplay of *Star Wars* helped make the film a reality, although in later years he professed to being disconcerted by the particular kind of fame it brought him. Guinness died on 5 August 2000, while *Attack of the Clones* was in production. 'He was one of the most talented and respected actors of his generation and brought an amazing range and versatility to his work,' said Lucas in tribute. 'The world has lost a great artist.'

SAMUEL L JACKSON
Mace Windu

Samuel Leroy Jackson was born in 1948 and had been acting for well over 20 years before his collaborations with writer/director Quentin Tarantino earned him both international stardom and a cult following. Following a brief appearance in the Tarantino-scripted *True Romance* (1993), Jackson went on to play Bible-quoting hitman Jules Winnfield in the classic *Pulp Fiction* (1994). He more recently worked with Tarantino on the Elmore Leonard adaptation *Jackie Brown* (1997), but can also be seen in *Jurassic Park* (1993), *Die Hard With a Vengeance* (1995) and *Shaft* (2000).

Jackson is a committed *Star Wars* fan, and saw the first movie on the day it was released in 1977. Twenty years later, he famously appealed to George Lucas during an appearance on Chris Evans's Channel 4 show *TFI Friday*, asking to be included in *The Phantom Menace*. The role of Mace Windu was written specially for him. Mace Windu has a bigger role to play in *Attack of the Clones*, and Jackson realised a long-held ambition when he finally got to swing a lightsaber.

Jackson modestly defers to Yoda when he describes Mace Windu as 'the second baddest person in the universe'. In *The Phantom Menace*, Mace was only briefly seen, evaluating Anakin's Force-sensitivity and conferring with Yoda over the boy's suitability for training. 'Just kinda chillin'', says Jackson. 'Being kind of wise and all knowing and just sitting around. But you know, I'm up on my feet and doing work now. It's going to be great. You're going to see another side of Mace Windu.'

Jackson was enthused by the new film's screenplay. 'There's romance for the kids who love romance stories. Young girls will be in love with Hayden Christensen, and the guys are going to be excited because Anakin's character is exciting, and Obi-Wan's character is exciting. The adults who saw *Star Wars* the first time will get the Harrison Ford feeling from this film, because there's that kind of irreverence and thrilling stuff going on. The guys who like action movies, they're going to like this movie because there's some really good action. It's going to appeal to a lot of people.'

In *Attack of the Clones*, Mace Windu remains a voice of reason on the Jedi Council, but he underestimates the threat posed by Count Dooku's Separatists. As war looms between the Republic's clone army and the Separatists' Battle Droids on Geonosis, however, Mace decides the time for diplomacy is over.

The fight scenes were carefully choreographed by stunt co-ordinator Nick Gillard. 'Nick is the man,' said Jackson during filming in Australia. 'This is my second go-round with him – he also did *Shaft*. Now he's doing lightsaber battles for us all, and a lot of Kendo stuff. I guess that, because I'm such a fan of Japanese samurai movies and I've watched a lot of Kendo fights, I'm doing pretty well at it. I don't do a lot of fancy sword-twirling or anything. I dispense people pretty quickly, use as little energy as possible. But I'm pretty bad.'

CHRISTOPHER LEE
Count Dooku

'I needed someone who could convey evil,' says George Lucas on the casting of Count Dooku. 'But in addition, I needed someone to bring stature, strength, and wisdom to the role. There was no doubt in my mind that Christopher Lee was the right person.'

'He's a terrific man,' says Ian McDiarmid of Lee, 'charming and amusing and highly sophisticated. I think he's particularly pleased to be in the movie because Peter Cushing, who was his good friend and working partner for so many years, was in the original *Star Wars* movie. I think that's somehow appropriate and quite moving.'

Christopher Lee CBE was born in London in 1922. After a career in Intelligence during the World War II, he decided to become an actor. 'My mother had major reservations,' he recalls. 'She said "Just think of all the appalling people you'll meet!"'

Since his screen debut in 1947's *Corridor of Mirrors*, Lee has appeared in over 200 movies. He is best known for the major commercial successes on his lengthy résumé – notably the Hammer Horror films that he regularly starred in between 1957 and 1976, and his role as James Bond's nemesis in *The Man With the Golden Gun* (1974). Lee's extensive television work includes a guest-starring role in the *Austria, March 1917* episode of *The Young Indiana Jones Chronicles*.

An experienced screen swordsman, Lee duelled Errol Flynn in *The Dark Avenger* (1954) and Oliver Reed in *The Three Musketeers* (1973). The experience came in useful for the scenes in which Dooku wields a suitably elegant lightsaber with a unique curved handle.

In recent years, Lee has appeared in some of the biggest films of his career – he had a cameo in Tim Burton's *Sleepy Hollow* (1999) and played Saruman the White in Peter Jackson's *The Lord of the Rings*. 'Appearing in *The Lord of the Rings* was like a dream come true for me,' he says, 'and it's wonderful to be part of *Star Wars* as well. Tim Burton, Peter Jackson, and George Lucas each have what I call the three 'i's – inspiration, imagination, and instinct. They know what they want, they know how to get it, and they care about what they're doing. That's really the characteristic common to all three. They care, they really care.'

PETER CUSHING
Grand Moff Tarkin

'I've often wondered what a 'Grand Moff' was,' said Peter Cushing of the character he played in *Star Wars*. 'It sounds like something that flew out of a cupboard.'

Star Wars came towards the end of a career that saw Cushing appear in nearly 100 films – over 20 with Christopher Lee – and some of the most acclaimed productions from the earliest years of British television. Cushing was overwhelmed when he saw *Star Wars*, and regretted that Tarkin's death prevented him from making return appearances in *The Empire Strikes Back* and *Return of the Jedi*.

Cushing was awarded the OBE in 1989 and gave his last performance in 1994 – narrating a documentary about Hammer films alongside Christopher Lee.

DOOKU OR BUST

Creating the bust of Count Dooku seen in the Jedi Archives was an arduous process. George Lucas asked that the bust be prepared in the style of French sculptor Auguste Rodin. 'Nothing negative about the guys that we actually had sculpting our busts,' says set decorator Peter Walpole, 'but they couldn't quite grasp what George wanted. We had three guys working on Christopher Lee busts. It wasn't a competition as such, although I guess it felt like one. Eventually one guy got close to it, and then George got his hands into the clay and started doing it himself! Which was a great relief to all of us, actually. He captured it immediately.'

IAN McDIARMID
Supreme Chancellor Palpatine

Ian McDiarmid was born in Dundee in 1947. When Emperor Palpatine was finally revealed in the flesh in *Return of the Jedi*, McDiarmid was cast in the role. Buried under layers of latex that took four hours to apply, McDiarmid brought the wizened despot to life with chilling effect.

McDiarmid has a noteworthy position in the *Attack of the Clones* ensemble – he is the only actor who has been hired to play a younger version of a human character he played in the original trilogy. As a result McDiarmid has reverse-engineered his portrayal of Palpatine. Having already shown us the decrepit Emperor, he is re-creating the same character in his Machiavellian middle age. There are traces of the old Emperor's snarling voice in the more sonorous tones of Supreme Chancellor Palpatine, but other than that McDiarmid is virtually unrecognisable as the character's younger self.

In summer 2002, Ian McDiarmid's artistic directorship of the London's Almeida Theatre, which he shares with Jonathan Kent, will come an end. Over the last 12 years, McDiarmid and Kent have transformed the former music hall into one of Britain's most vibrant and acclaimed venues. Under the auspices of McDiarmid and Kent, the Almeida has won more than 45 awards, including Laurence Olivier and Evening Standard Awards for outstanding achievement. The theatre has premiered new plays by Edward Albee, David Hare, and Harold Pinter; hosted a daring programme of European and classical works; and attracted such star names as Juliette Binoche, Nicole Kidman, Kevin Spacey, and Ralph Fiennes.

Intense speculation surrounds McDiarmid and Kent's career plans, but for now McDiarmid is happy to devote some time to the evil character he first played almost 20 years ago. 'Everything Palpatine does is an act of pure hypocrisy,' says McDiarmid, 'and that's interesting to play. I suppose it's rather like playing Iago. All the characters in the play – including Othello, until the end – think that "Honest Iago" is a decent guy doing his job, and he's quite liked. But at the same time there's a tremendous evil subconscious in operation.'

McDiarmid had only three days to learn his lines before his first scene in *Attack of the Clones*. 'I was midair on this pod,' he remembers, 'there was a camera pointing at me, and I was addressing crosses as markers rather than real actors. It was a new crew and there were new actors entering the *Star Wars* universe for the first time. All of those things were flying through my mind, and it was quite scary. However, I've learned that you can use that kind of fear if you can control it. The first few days were about taking control of that fear.'

British theatre awaits McDiarmid's next move almost as eagerly as *Star Wars* fans await Palpatine's final transformation in Episode III.

MARK HAMILL
Luke Skywalker

In *Return of the Jedi*, Ian McDiarmid shared some unforgettable scenes with Mark Hamill, the actor who became a hero to millions as Luke Skywalker in the original *Star Wars* trilogy.

Hamill began his career with a small role in television's *The Bill Cosby Show* in 1970, but didn't find fame until he played Luke, the farm boy who rescued a princess, in *Star Wars*. Hamill was involved in a car crash following *Star Wars* and underwent extensive reconstructive surgery prior to filming *The Empire Strikes Back*. Following *Return of the Jedi*, he appeared in acclaimed stage productions of *Amadeus* and *The Elephant Man*. More recently, he has voiced The Joker in *Batman: The Animated Series* and guest-starred in *The Simpsons*.

FRANK OZ
Yoda

Frank Oz was born in Hereford in 1944 but moved to New York when he was 19 to begin puppeteering with Jim Henson and the Muppets. When Henson launched the classic children's show *Sesame Street* in 1969, Oz created some of the most memorable characters, such as Bert, Grover, and Cookie Monster.

Sesame Street continued to grow in popularity, and in 1976 Henson created the prime time hit *The Muppet Show*. Oz voiced the characters Animal, Fozzie Bear, and Sam the Eagle. His best remembered

contribution to the series was, however, arguably its most popular character – the brash wannabe, Miss Piggy.

Oz's skills as a puppeteer and voice artist made him an obvious choice to bring the wizened Jedi Master Yoda to life in *The Empire Strikes Back* and *Return of the Jedi*. George Lucas asked Oz to reprise the role in *The Phantom Menace*, and Oz realised the demanding scenes with assistance from fellow puppeteers Kathy Smee (Yoda's right arm), Don Austen (Yoda's ears), and David Greenaway (Yoda's eyes). 'You can't be trying to do your own thing,' said Smee. 'Frank performs the character. He *is* the character. We just try to give him freedom, to work with his performance, to flow with it. Because no matter what we rehearse, Frank will always do something a little more, a little different for the real take.'

For one scene in *The Phantom Menace*, in which Yoda was seen walking across a room, the character was computer generated by ILM. Yoda is entirely computer generated for the duration of *Attack of the Clones*, enabling him to participate in physically dynamic scenes, such as the duel with Count Dooku, for the first time. Oz continues to provide Yoda's distinctive voice, expertly interpreting the curiously jumbled syntax that has made the character famous.

Oz continues to maintain his links with *Star Wars* and the Muppets, but for the last 20 years has enjoyed another career as a successful film director. His most recent successes have included *In & Out* (1997), *Bowfinger* (1999) and *The Score* (2001).

ANTHONY DANIELS
C-3PO

Although he has also appeared in such disparate productions as *I Bought a Vampire Motorcycle* (1990) and the *Prime Suspect* series, Anthony Daniels admits that fussy Protocol Droid C-3PO is now an omnipresent part of his life.

In *Star Wars*, Daniels endured extreme discomfort inside the golden suit, which became progressively lighter and easier to assemble in *The Empire Strikes Back* and *Return of the Jedi*. When the character was shown in *The Phantom Menace*, it resembled a skeletal assembly of nuts and bolts and was operated by a puppeteer. At least Daniels was on hand to once more provide the precise and particularly English tones that have become associated with the character, however he looks.

When asked if he has any idea what C-3PO has been up to since *The Phantom Menace*, Anthony Daniels is ready with a humorous response. 'He's been learning macramé,' says the actor with a straight face. 'He's been knitting himself a suit to cover up his nudity, and earning the money to buy the wool by working as a bingo caller at Mos Eisley.'

In *Attack of the Clones*, C-3PO's golden suit was hand-painted in a new colour scheme by Justin Dix (who later made an Oscar-sized facsimile as a present to Daniels from the team).

'The greatest challenge for me was to squeeze back into the suit,' says Daniels. 'I got down to one meal a day, stopped eating desserts and cut out the delicious Australian wine. And I was in the gym at 5.00 am every morning. The pay-off came when I just slipped back into the old thing.'

While filming the Lars Homestead scenes in Tunisia, Daniels recalled the shoot for the original *Star Wars* in 1976. 'I realised that George and I were the only people who had stood there before, 25 years ago. I was reflecting on this when Gavin Bocquet came up to me and asked me how I felt. I told him it was like I'd never been away.'

Daniels also played C-3PO in all three *Star Wars* radio adaptations, *The Star Wars Holiday Special*, and appeared on *The Muppet Show* and *Sesame Street*. Despite making such an indelible impression, Daniels has had to wait 25 years for his face to be seen in a *Star Wars* film. In *Attack of the Clones* he can be glimpsed as Dannl Faytonni, a conman disguised as a Lieutenant of the Republic Guard in Coruscant's Outlander gambling club.

KENNY BAKER
R2-D2

Entertainer Kenny Baker has made a virtue of his 3' 8" height in an eclectic career that has included appearances in pantomimes, *The Elephant Man* (1980), and just about everything in between.

Baker is called upon to animate R2-D2 for close-ups and other scenes in which the droid is not radio-controlled. Ten R2-D2 props were used on *Attack of the Clones* – eight radio-controlled units, one unarticulated stunt model and a hollow prop that Baker operated in one scene.

JIMMY SMITS
Bail Organa

The name Organa has long been familiar to Star Wars fans as the adopted surname of Princess Leia in the original trilogy. Much has been written about Leia's guardian, and the heroic role he played in the Clone Wars prior to his death on Alderaan, but his face had never been seen – until now.

Senator Bail Organa is played by Emmy award-winner Jimmy Smits, who for many years was one of the best-known faces on American television. Smits was born in Brooklyn, New York, but raised in Puerto Rico, where he learned to speak Spanish. Smits is best known for his leading roles in the drama series LA Law and NYPD Blue.

PERNILLA AUGUST
Shmi Skywalker

Swedish actress Pernilla August has worked with such distinguished directors as Ingmar Bergman and Lasse Hallström, but was relatively unknown outside Europe until her appearance as Anakin's mother in *The Phantom Menace*.

Rick McCallum remembered August from her two appearances in episodes of *The Young Indiana Jones Chronicles*. On those occasions, she had spoken Italian and German – *The Phantom Menace* was the first English-speaking role of her career. August appeared in some of the film's most emotional moments, revealing that Anakin had no father and later saying a sad farewell to her only son.

August went on to star in NBC's *Mary, Mother of Jesus* opposite Christian Bale. The 43-year-old actress now seems resigned to the fact that casting directors seem to regard her as the ideal choice to play virginal mothers.

August makes only a brief appearance in *Attack of the Clones*, but she has a starring role in some of the most harrowing scenes in this – or any other – *Star Wars* movie. She was introduced to her 'new' son Hayden Christensen, who took over the role of Anakin from Jake Lloyd, during studio filming in Sydney. 'He was so sweet and very good,' she says, praising Christensen's anguished performance. 'He has the same warmth and kindness of Jake.'

August retains only happy memories of her time on Tatooine. 'To be part of *Star Wars* is like a dream. For me, it really does feel like a dream, because it's something I visit and then I go back to my normal life. It is like a candy I have in my pocket, and I can put it in my mouth and just dream about it whenever I want.'

SILAS CARSON
Ki-Adi-Mundi and Nute Gunray

Silas Carson resumes his portrayal of two of the more unusual characters from *The Phantom Menace*. Carson endured many hours in the make-up chair while prosthetics transformed him into either wise Jedi Master Ki-Adi-Mundi or devious Neimodian Nute Gunray.

The versatile Carson also provides the distinctive voices for both characters, emphasising the Jedi's wise and noble qualities while ensuring that the cowardly Nute sounds suitably snivelling.

Far from the *Star Wars* universe, Carson has a regular role as an anaesthetist in the successful ITV medical drama *A&E*.

ANDY SECOMBE
Watto

Andy Secombe, whose father was the legendary Sir Harry, once again provides the fruity tones of disreputable Toydarian Watto.

As in Episode I, Andy stood in for his character on set and interacted with Hayden Christensen for the scene in which Anakin asks his former owner if he knows Shmi's whereabouts.

When he's not resisting Jedi mind tricks, Andy runs Lunchtime Productions, a company that specialises in animated shows.

AHMED BEST
Jar Jar Binks

The dexterous Ahmed Best was the physical realisation of Jar Jar Binks during the filming of *Attack of the Clones*. Once ILM had created and added the digital character, Best completed his work providing Jar Jar's distinctive voice.

Best was a member of percussive theatre group Stomp when casting director Robin Gurland spotted him and noted he had the necessary skills to choreograph the amphibian's clumsy gait and slapstick mishaps. Best was delighted to win the role. '*Star Wars* was the first movie I ever saw,' he says. 'I was three years old when it came out. I vividly remember walking into the theatre, sitting down, and watching the entire movie. And I remember it just blowing my mind.'

Ahmed is required to wear a body suit and a 'hat' of Jar Jar's head to help his fellow actors maintain the correct eyeline for the character waiting to be digitally superimposed.

In *Attack of the Clones*, it is a very different Jar Jar we see during his brief scenes on Coruscant. Best was aware that Jar Jar had aged ten years since the events of *The Phantom Menace*, and worked on conveying his increased age and experience while retaining the characteristics that endeared him to so many of *Star Wars*' younger fans. 'That was probably my biggest challenge in Episode II – trying to make Jar Jar seem mature, without taking away any sense of his fun, and any of his child-like sense of discovery.'

Best's real face can be seen briefly in *Attack of the Clones* – he plays one Achk Med-Beq, an accomplice to Dannl Faytonni (Anthony Daniels), in the Outlander gambling club.

'You're going to pay for all the Jedi you killed today, Dooku.'

A PITCHED BATTLE rages between the clone troopers and the Battle Droids outside the arena. Meanwhile, in a secret hangar, Count Dooku readies his ship for the flight from Geonosis.

Obi-Wan and Anakin disembark from their gunship at the hangar's entrance, and Obi-Wan tells his Padawan they should tackle the Count together. But Anakin believes Padmé may have been killed, and is blinded by his rage. He rushes forwards alone.

Dooku simply smiles and repels Anakin with a shattering burst of Sith lightning. Anakin is thrown across the room and lands in a heap, semi-conscious.

Obi-Wan and Dooku thrust and parry, but Dooku is the superior swordsman and forces Obi-Wan further and further back. Obi-Wan is struck first in the shoulder, and then in the thigh, and finally loses his lightsaber. Dooku raises his own weapon to deliver the final blow, when Anakin springs to the defence of his helpless Master. Anakin raises his lightsaber to Dooku's and the two blades lock.

Dooku is momentarily caught off-balance. Obi-Wan uses the Force to toss his lightsaber to Anakin, who advances on Dooku with a weapon in each hand. Dooku then launches a spirited resistance, which culminates when he severs Anakin's arm at the elbow. Anakin collapses in agony.

Both Obi-Wan and Anakin are defeated, but one further obstacle stands between Dooku and his rendezvous with Darth Sidious. Through the thick smoke appears the unmistakable figure of Yoda. He stares defiantly up at his former Padawan and ignites his lightsaber.

This particular battle is far from over....

Index

Fictional characters are indexed by their first names, ie 'Luke Skywalker'.

ACKNOWLEDGMENTS

My grateful thanks to Paul Bufton and Samantha Kite for their support, and to Jake Lingwood and Claire Kingston at Ebury Press for the tea and sympathy. Thanks also to Dan Newman for doing a superb job with the design and knowing how to drive on the wrong side of the road.

Special thanks to everyone at Industrial Light & Magic, JAK Productions, and Lucas Licensing who helped with the preparation of this book. I am particularly indebted to editor Jonathan Rinzler for the home cooking; art director Iain Morris for sharing his memories of the golden years of music hall; and Chris 'Suit you, sir' Cerasi for the comic interludes. Thanks also to the following folk at Lucasfilm and ILM: Ryan Church; Dan Gregoire; Wendy Menara; Fred Meyers; Erik Tiemens; and Judith Weaver.

Finally, my thanks to the following people for their valuable contributions: Scott Chernoff; Anthony Daniels; Pablo Hidalgo; Andrew Kemp; James King; Christopher Lee; Iain Lowson; and Fiona Macmillan.